Kingdom Formation

"Giving voice to the deep anxieties in our age made all the more pressing by those of us who confess Jesus as Lord over it all, Robert Snitko points readers toward an answer: the kingdom of God. With a conversational style, Snitko not only clearly lays out the scriptural vision but also plots a way forward for readers to participate in it. This is an inspiring book that equips readers to begin to live in light of God's goodness and power."

—AMY PEELER, professor of New Testament, Wheaton College

"Robert Snitko unpacks the wealth of biblical teachings concerning life in God's eternal kingdom and gives us a vision of what our lives become when we receive Jesus and all that he provides. The exciting fact is, those who have received him, are already living in his kingdom where peace, joy, and hope are our inheritance. *Kingdom Formation* is a celebration of this reality and a helpful guide for those who yearn to experience life to the fullest in Christ."

—SANJAY MERCHANT, professor of theology, Moody Bible Institute

"*Kingdom Formation* is an in-depth exploration of the life God calls every follower to embody. The individualized exploration for each fruit of the Spirit is insightful and easily applied. The call for kingdom unity resonates with any heart hungry for God's way to manifest. Simple, clear, compelling, and worth every minute."

—KEN NABI, regional president, Converge Great Lakes

"Robert Snitko has the audacity to believe that eternal life is more than just going to be with Jesus in heaven when we die. He can be this audacious, of course, because he has read and loves the Bible—the Bible which tells us on every page that salvation is not a matter of life after death, but of entering this very moment into the life that has conquered death in the crucifixion and resurrection of the Son of God and the pouring out of the Holy Spirit."

—ANDREW ARNDT, lead pastor, New Life East

"This book is a great read for those wanting to experience more of what kingdom living looks like on this side of eternity. I'm grateful for the fresh insight and inspiration it gives to those desiring to live for Jesus in such a time as this. I'm thankful for Robert Snitko's love for Jesus and commitment to God's word as I've known him for many years and observed it firsthand. May we all experience more of the hope this book offers!"

—RON ZAPPIA, founding and senior pastor, Highpoint Church

Kingdom Formation

Being Transformed for Life on Earth as It Is in Heaven

ROBERT SNITKO

WIPF & STOCK · Eugene, Oregon

KINGDOM FORMATION
Being Transformed for Life on Earth as It Is in Heaven

Copyright © 2023 Robert Snitko. All rights reserved. Except for brief quotations in critical publications or reviews, no part of this book may be reproduced in any manner without prior written permission from the publisher. Write: Permissions, Wipf and Stock Publishers, 199 W. 8th Ave., Suite 3, Eugene, OR 97401.

Wipf & Stock
An Imprint of Wipf and Stock Publishers
199 W. 8th Ave., Suite 3
Eugene, OR 97401

www.wipfandstock.com

PAPERBACK ISBN: 979-8-3852-0515-8
HARDCOVER ISBN: 979-8-3852-0516-5
EBOOK ISBN: 979-8-3852-0517-2

Italics in Scripture quotations have been added by the author for emphasis.

Unless otherwise stated, Scripture quotations have been taken from the Christian Standard Bible®, copyright © 2017 by Holman Bible Publishers. Used by permission. Christian Standard Bible® and CSB® are federally registered trademarks of Holman Bible Publishers.

Scriptures quotations marked NIV have been taken from the Holy Bible, New International Version®, NIV®. Copyright © 1973, 1978, 1984, 2011 by Biblica, Inc.™ Used by permission of Zondervan. All rights reserved worldwide.

Other Books by Robert Snitko

A Love We Don't Deserve:
Finding Freedom in God's Grace

God is Not Black-and-White:
Seeking Unity in a Theologically Diverse Church

Lessons Learned from Jonah:
Meditations on God's Restoring Grace

For Mags, Ryle, Liv, and Ever

Your kingdom come. Your will be done on earth as it is in heaven.
—MATT 6:10

Contents

Acknowledgments xi

Preface xiii

Introduction xv

PART ONE: *A Kingdom Spirituality*

Chapter One | Homeward Bound 3

Chapter Two | Spiritual Vitality for Kingdom Life 14

PART TWO: *A Kingdom Lifestyle*

Chapter Three | Kingdom Love 35

Chapter Four | Kingdom Unity 47

PART THREE: *A Kingdom Experience*

Chapter Five | Kingdom Presence 63

Chapter Six | Kingdom Spirit 91

Chapter Seven | Kingdom Hope 99

Chapter Eight | Kingdom Growth 109

Epilogue 119

Biblical Texts for Further Study on Kingdom 122

Bibliography 125

Acknowledgments

MY BRIDE, MAGS: You have ventured with me on this journey called life for over a decade. We have had so many conversations throughout the last decade that have helped shape who I am today. Thank you for showing the incredible love of Christ toward me and others. You humbly reflect and represent Jesus's call to love God and our neighbors well. This is one of the most infectious things about you. You have demonstrated so beautifully what kingdom living looks like here on earth.

Ryle, Liv, and Ever: Thank you for making me a father. The things I have learned about the love of God by simply being your dad have been life-changing. I praise God for you three.

Larry Sheahan: We did not spend much time together in ministry, but the time we did spend was exceptional. You led me and taught me so well. I've said it before and I'll say it again: what I learned under your leadership is more than I have learned in the previous decade of ministry. I am forever grateful for your legacy at Faith Fellowship and your influence on my life.

Faith Fellowship: After many years in different churches, I cannot stress enough how Faith Fellowship truly feels like a healthy and growing family. How you embraced my family into a new community in 2020 said so much about how remarkable the people are here. It is a joy to serve you as your pastor. May God continue to grow each one of you into a kingdom people as you trust in him with all of life's details. I look forward to all that God is going to do here in the coming years.

Preface

I AM OBSESSED WITH coffee. Every morning that I wake up, one of my first thoughts is, how can I get my hands on a cup of coffee as soon as possible? Whenever I visit cities throughout the US, I am always looking up what coffee shops I can visit. There is a wonderful coffee shop where I live now that I absolutely cannot get enough of. But sometimes when I come in for a cup of coffee, I operate like a robot. I walk in, say hello, grab my coffee, and the barista will say, "Thanks for coming." My response, without even knowing it, goes something like this, "You too." Whoops. I am the one who went to the coffee shop; they were simply there for work. This is sometimes the symptom of repetition. When we do something enough times, we may find ourselves not being in the moment. Instead, we find ourselves operating in what I like to call "robot mode."

When I hear or read the words "on earth as it is in heaven," these words remind me of the constant reciting of the Lord's Prayer growing up. I have encountered these words so many times that when they come out of my mouth, I feel like I am reciting them in robot mode. The same is true when I read them on the pages of Scripture. One morning, I found myself pondering these words and they hit me differently than usual. I kept thinking to myself, what does this mean for me? How can I be formed through this statement in my spiritual journey with Jesus?

I didn't think that I would be writing a book on spiritual formation anytime soon. I was an exhausted writer who had just finished a doctorate in spiritual formation. There was certainly more than enough writing done there to exhaust someone. As I sat there on a summer morning, I kept thinking to myself, what would it look like if followers of Jesus lived their lives on earth through the lens of the kingdom of God? Instead of thinking that one day we will be in eternity, what if we started thinking about today through the lens of eternity? As these questions permeated

Preface

my mind, I couldn't help but write down the reflections that the Spirit put on my heart. Before I knew it, a book was forming right before my very eyes. This is what you hold in your hands. I began working on this project because the Lord began to reveal to me the importance of being formed for the kingdom while still being a resident here on earth. Our time on earth is short. Our time in the kingdom will be eternal. We are given an opportunity to dwell as pilgrims on earth while growing and developing into who God intended us to be. Imagine if we would give God room to form us on earth as it is in heaven. This could change everything. The way we handled fear, anxiety, worry, chaos—just to name a few—would completely change. We would not see things from the lens of the hopelessness that exists in this world; instead, we would see things from a kingdom perspective, knowing that God is doing something in our midst, even though we may not see it in the moment. We would be able to reflect God's glory to those around us. We would be able to bridge the gap between who we are and who we were created to be. We would become faithful followers of Jesus who look less like the world around us and more like the person of Jesus. Perhaps, followers of Jesus would get less caught up in the pettiness of church drama and truly have a heart and desire to see lives transformed by the power of the gospel. This is what *Kingdom Formation* is all about. This book will encourage followers of Jesus to grow. Grow in their spiritual formation as kingdom people. We have been given one chance at life on earth. Let's use it to live like kingdom people.

Introduction

I have had so many thoughts ruminating in my mind for the last four years regarding the state of the world, the state of Christianity, and the state of the church. The thoughts were so clustered in my mind that I didn't know what to think about it all. My family took a major leap of faith in the fall of 2020, where we left everything we knew for a place that was foreign to us. We made a move from Chicago to central Wisconsin. We had no ties to central Wisconsin and had never visited here; it was simply a call from the Lord that we felt compelled to answer with a hesitant yes. I remember during this time of transition for us, the COVID-19 pandemic nearly shut down the entire world, a very divisive election cycle transpired in the US, and the church of Jesus Christ seemed to be in shambles. What was going on? What was happening? Why was there so much division, disunity, and frustration? Why were Christians fleeing from the church? Was God still working and moving in our midst? Or had God given up on the church and the world? These were all of the questions that were taking over my thoughts. And this was all happening while God was very clearly leading my family to a new location for a new ministry assignment. Nothing was making sense.

So we moved. From big city to small-town life. Everything was new. Everything was different. And the questions remained in my mind. What in the world is going on? My anxiety was at an all-time high, and I did not know what the future would hold. Then, I was confronted with the Gospel writer Matthew, who so eloquently records Jesus's words from the Sermon on the Mount:

> Therefore I tell you: Don't worry about your life, what you will eat or what you will drink; or about your body, what you will wear. Isn't life more than food and the body more than clothing? Consider the birds of the sky: They don't sow or reap or gather

into barns, yet your heavenly Father feeds them. Aren't you worth more than they? Can any of you add one moment to his life span by worrying? And why do you worry about clothes? Observe how the wildflowers of the field grow: They don't labor or spin thread. Yet I tell you that not even Solomon in all his splendor was adorned like one of these. If that's how God clothes the grass of the field, which is here today and thrown into the furnace tomorrow, won't he do much more for you—you of little faith? So don't worry, saying, "What will we eat?" or "What will we drink?" or "What will we wear?" For the Gentiles eagerly seek all these things, and your heavenly Father knows that you need them. But seek first the kingdom of God and his righteousness, and all these things will be provided for you. Therefore don't worry about tomorrow, because tomorrow will worry about itself. Each day has enough trouble of its own. (Matt 6:25–34)

I thought, wow. This grounded me. This brought me back to where my thoughts needed to be. I do not have to be anxious about everything that is going on around me. Jesus will take care of those things. I just need to take it one day at a time and rely on the grace and mercies of God, which are new every morning (Lam 3:22–23). But there was something even deeper in Matthew's Gospel that caught onto me that I just could not shed. Jesus says, "But seek first the kingdom of God and his righteousness, and all these things will be provided for you" (Matt 6:33). Jesus talks about all of the worries in our lives, and then he presents a strong contrast when he uses the word "but." Yes, there are many worries, fears, and anxieties, *but* we must be a people who seek first the kingdom of God.

KINGDOM PERSPECTIVE

Jesus's words that exclaimed "Seek first the kingdom of God" changed my life. This was revolutionary for me. I began to look at the astronomical amount of kingdom language that is used throughout the New Testament, and how often Jesus would talk about the kingdom. Even when it came to the Lord's Prayer in Matt 6, we see Jesus teaching his disciples to pray using the language "Your kingdom come. Your will be done on earth as it is in heaven" (Matt 6:10). The task of a follower of Jesus is to live a life that is kingdom minded. We are to have a kingdom focus. When our minds are focused on the things of this world, we will quickly begin to fall into the trap of unending anxiety, fear, and worry. When we put our hope in the

Introduction

security of this world, we will only find ourselves at a loss. When we put our hope in a government and think it will provide the help and healing that our nation needs, we again will be disappointed. When we do not seek first the kingdom of God, we will perpetually find ourselves in a cycle of anger, fear, and obsession over the wrong things. We are in this world, but we are not of this world. Followers of Jesus are called to be kingdom people. A people who represent our King, the one and only King, and his name is Jesus. When Jesus truly becomes the King and Lord of our life, it is only then that we will have eyes to see that nothing in this world will ever please us beyond a mere temporary fulfillment. When we long for the things of this world to bring us joy and satisfaction, we slowly begin to dethrone the Christ who gave us his life so that we would have life in him. We simply choose lifelessness. When everything in the world seems like it is falling apart, it is because it is indeed falling apart. This is not our home. We are sojourners, just passing by, until we finally arrive home.

As all these thoughts have been sifting through my mind, I have been jotting down various things God has been teaching me. I found myself passionate about the kingdom of God and what kingdom life looks like here on earth. That is why I felt compelled to write this book. I wanted to invite you, the reader, a precious child of God, to think through some of these things with me. I rejoice in the thought that one day we will be worshiping our glorious God together, in unity, forever and ever. So buckle up as we dive into what it means to be kingdom people.

PART ONE: A Kingdom Spirituality

CHAPTER 1

Homeward Bound

So if you have been raised with Christ, seek the things above, where Christ is, seated at the right hand of God. Set your minds on things above, not on earthly things. For you died, and your life is hidden with Christ in God. When Christ, who is your life, appears, then you also will appear with him in glory.

—Col 3:1–4

I HAD THE REMARKABLE privilege to go on a mission trip to the country of Zambia. Before the trip, I had never flown overseas. If I'm being honest with you, I was terrified to fly over the second-largest pond in the world, The Atlantic Ocean. But my mind was made up, and it was time to begin the journey. On the way to Lusaka, Zambia, we had to make a connecting flight to Dubai. If you didn't know, Dubai is the home to the world's largest skyscraper, the Burj Khalifa. I thought to myself, there is no way we are going to Dubai, and I am not setting foot in this building. I hail from the great city of Chicago and am fond of large buildings. At one point living in a city where I could see the skyline out my window, the idea of seeing the Burj Khalifa reminded me of home. So we landed, and there it was. The most beautiful building I had ever seen. My group decided that we would pay a visit and see this beautiful architecture. Once we got to the Burj Khalifa, we went to the top. It was breathtaking. I was taking in the views and admiring everything that was around me. The experience reminded me of being back home in Chicago. Even though I was thousands of miles away from home, I caught glimpses of what home felt like.

We all have a place that we call home. A place where there is comfort. A place where everything feels familiar. A place where we can go, be, and rest. A sacred place. After a long day of work, home is a place waiting for us to enter into and dwell. A place that we call our own. A place where we belong. A home is a place that is our nucleus. The central hub, where all of our belongings are meant to be stored. When we leave home for work, vacation, a meeting, a lunch out, a fancy coffee break, or for whatever other reason you decide, we hope to come back home once again.

A BROKEN KINGDOM

When I think of home, I think of the kingdom of God. I think of the place which a Christian's heart longs for. A place where every tear will be wiped away. Where death will be no more. Where grief, crying, and pain will be no more (Rev 21:4). This kingdom is a place where we will be in the eternal presence of our Savior and Lord, together, with other followers of Jesus. This place will be filled with glory and praise forevermore. The kingdom is our home. The kingdom is our aspired destiny. But what happens when we find ourselves in a place that is filled with chaos, hate, discrimination, war, turmoil, greed, lies, lust, pain, suffering, and death—to name just a few? What do we do when we long for heaven on earth while still participating in the present-day reality of living in a broken and hurting world? As followers of Jesus, I believe we are called to be *kingdom people*. A people who participate, along with the Trinitarian God—Father, Son, and Holy Spirit—in ushering in the beauty and reconciliation of what kingdom life can look like here on earth. Praise be to God that we can access his authoritative and Holy Scriptures to help guide us in this kind of life. A life that starts and ends with the kingdom. A life that recognizes that we are here for just a moment, and then we move on. Or as James so wittingly put it, "Yet you do not know what tomorrow will bring—what your life will be! For you are like vapor that appears for a little while, then vanishes" (Jas 4:14). Our lives here on earth are temporary, yet so often, we live like we are immortal. It is only when pain and suffering enter into our lives that we begin to realize that this life is not how it's supposed to be. Things are not right.

GARDEN BEAUTY AND BROKENNESS

The Creator of the universe decided to make a beautiful planet that was formless and empty (Gen 1:2). He spoke light into existence (Gen 1:3). He filled the planet with land and sea (Gen 1:9–10). He produced vegetation and trees that bear fruit (Gen 1:11–13). He separated the light from the darkness and called them "day and night" (Gen 1:14–19). The beautiful waters were filled with living creatures, and birds filled the skies (Gen 1:20–23). He then filled the land with livestock and creatures that move on the ground. He filled it with wild animals, each according to its kind (Gen 1:24–25). All of this was good. It was oh-so-very-good. God delighted in what he had created, but it didn't end there. The book of Genesis records:

> Then God said, "Let us make man in our image, according to our likeness. They will rule the fish of the sea, the birds of the sky, the livestock, the whole earth, and the creatures that crawl on the earth." So God created man in his own image; he created him in the image of God; he created them male and female. God blessed them, and God said to them, "Be fruitful, multiply, fill the earth, and subdue it. Rule the fish of the sea, the birds of the sky, and every creature that crawls on the earth." God also said, "Look, I have given you every seed-bearing plant on the surface of the entire earth and every tree whose fruit contains seed. This will be food for you, for all the wildlife of the earth, for every bird of the sky, and for every creature that crawls on the earth—everything having the breath of life in it—I have given every green plant for food." And it was so. God saw all that he had made, and it was very good indeed. (Gen 1:26–31)

Humankind was created to represent and reflect the image of God. God had created all things good, and adding to that goodness was humankind. After creating humankind, God specifically instructed humankind, "You are free to eat from any tree of the garden, but you must not eat from the tree of the knowledge of good and evil, for on the day you eat from it, you will certainly die" (Gen 2:16–17). Everything in creation was good except for the fact that man was alone (Gen 2:18). So God created an *ezer* for man. *Ezer* is the Hebrew word for "helper," and it indicates "the one who supplies strength in the area that is lacking in 'the helped.'"[1] Now man did not have to be alone. There was companionship, and there was a

---

1. *ESV Study Bible*, 57.

relationship—which corresponded to the image of God. The Trinitarian God would now have a relationship with his image-bearers. There was beauty in the garden.

After some time, humanity was faced with temptation. The crafty and cunning Satan made his way into the beautiful garden that God had made and began to twist the words of God. He was so crafty that he was successful in misleading and misguiding humanity to rebel against God (Gen 3:1–7). The forbidden fruit was indulged upon, and the course of human history changed. Sin entered into the world. What once was a beautiful and harmonious relationship between God and his creation became a severed and broken relationship. The beautiful garden experienced brokenness. Things would not be the same anymore because humankind chose the creation over the Creator. Evil over good. Death over life. What once felt like home had now become a foreign place.

THE MODERN GARDEN

The modern garden—or the modern world—does a good job of replicating what the garden's brokenness looked like. We have a Creator God who is deeply personal and heavily involved in our day-to-day lives. A God who longs and desires to be near to us (Jas 4:8). A God who is jealous of his image-bearers (Exod 34:14). A God who loves his precious people so much and desires that they would have an abundant life (John 10:10). But that tree in the garden that is so enticing—the tree that overpromises and under-delivers—that tree continues to lure humankind toward itself while leaving people empty of fulfillment and satisfaction. That tree lures us toward materialism, money, promotions, security, the approval of others, a government that will allegedly save us, and false happiness. We can look back and say that we haven't learned all that much since the garden. We are still fragile people who are easily swayed. We are still easily persuaded by the things of this world, all while continuing to neglect the most important relationship that we can have—a relationship with our Creator. The one who made us. The one who looks at us and sees the image of himself. And we respond by marring that image, over and over again. We inevitably continue to indulge in self-fulfillment, hoping to find some meaning and purpose in something. We choose to bow down before the idols of this world. Chasing after the wind, all while losing ourselves in it all.

CHASING AFTER THE WIND

Eugene Peterson, in his book *A Long Obedience in the Same Direction*, writes, "An excellent way to test people's values is to observe what we do when we don't have to do anything."[2] Being put in a situation like this gives us insight into where our priorities are. When we have nothing to do, it can be easy to be tempted and lured by the forbidden fruit. The fruit that dupes us into thinking that the things of this world are high priority and of absolute importance in our lives. This can cause us to chase after the wind. To pursue things that are empty and void. In the book of Ecclesiastes, the author often uses the terminology of "chasing after the wind." This idea of chasing after the wind suggests that we are pursuing futility. Chasing after the things in life that seemingly exist, though they are only temporary. I will let the author of Ecclesiastes tell the story:

> I said to myself, "Go ahead, I will test you with pleasure; enjoy what is good." But it turned out to be futile. I said about laughter, "It is madness," and about pleasure, "What does this accomplish?" I explored with my mind the pull of wine on my body—my mind still guiding me with wisdom—and how to grasp folly, until I could see what is good for people to do under heaven during the few days of their lives. I increased my achievements. I built houses and planted vineyards for myself. I made gardens and parks for myself and planted every kind of fruit tree in them. I constructed reservoirs for myself from which to irrigate a grove of flourishing trees. I acquired male and female servants and had slaves who were born in my house. I also owned livestock—large herds and flocks—more than all who were before me in Jerusalem. I also amassed silver and gold for myself, and the treasure of kings and provinces. I gathered male and female singers for myself, and many concubines, the delights of men. So I became great and surpassed all who were before me in Jerusalem; my wisdom also remained with me. All that my eyes desired, I did not deny them. I did not refuse myself any pleasure, for I took pleasure in all my struggles. This was my reward for all my struggles. When I considered all that I had accomplished and what I had labored to achieve, I found everything to be futile and a pursuit of the wind. There was nothing to be gained under the sun. (Eccl 2:1–11)

The conclusion that the writer of the book of Ecclesiastes gets to is that pursuing the things of this world is meaningless. Pleasure, wealth, wisdom,

---

2. Peterson, *Long Obedience*, 44.

and work—chasing after these things will leave us senseless and empty. The things of this world can certainly be enjoyed, but chasing after them over the Creator will leave us void. When all is said and done, it will get us nowhere. The only thing that we hang on to is our relationship with our Lord. I have heard it said once that you don't see a hearse pulling a U-Haul. This is a great image of this temporal life on earth. What we must long for is eternity. Long for that which lasts. What is being done here on earth as it is in heaven? How can God show us that we must not chase after the wind of this world but seek first the kingdom of God? Followers of Jesus are homeward bound. Everyone gets to their destination at different times. That is why we must not chase after the wind and cling to Jesus.

A NEW CREATION

Maybe we have found ourselves chasing after the wind. Maybe we are in a place where we realize that we are not living a kingdom life on earth as it is in heaven. Or maybe we are in a place where we just need to hit a reset button in our faith walk and reorient ourselves back toward our Creator. Wherever we may find ourselves, it is important to be a people who are homeward bound.

Saul of Tarsus was not a good man. He was a persecutor of Christians. He ravaged the early Christian church and threw men and women into prison (Acts 8:1–3). He threatened followers of Jesus (Acts 9:1–2). As someone who would follow Jesus in that day and age, it would be easy to say that being in the presence of Saul of Tarsus was not something that was coveted. That is, until his life was flipped upside down. Saul was on his way to Damascus, and Luke, the writer of the book of Acts, records this:

> As he traveled and was nearing Damascus, a light from heaven suddenly flashed around him. Falling to the ground, he heard a voice saying to him, "Saul, Saul, why are you persecuting me?" "Who are you, Lord?" Saul said. "I am Jesus, the one you are persecuting," he replied. "But get up and go into the city, and you will be told what you must do." The men who were traveling with him stood speechless, hearing the sound but seeing no one. Saul got up from the ground, and though his eyes were open, he could see nothing. So they took him by the hand and led him into Damascus. He was unable to see for three days and did not eat or drink. There was a disciple in Damascus named Ananias, and the Lord said to him in a vision, "Ananias." "Here I am, Lord," he replied.

"Get up and go to the street called Straight," the Lord said to him, "to the house of Judas, and ask for a man from Tarsus named Saul, since he is praying there. In a vision he has seen a man named Ananias coming in and placing his hands on him so that he may regain his sight." "Lord," Ananias answered, "I have heard from many people about this man, how much harm he has done to your saints in Jerusalem. And he has authority here from the chief priests to arrest all who call on your name." But the Lord said to him, "Go, for this man is my chosen instrument to take my name to Gentiles, kings, and Israelites. I will show him how much he must suffer for my name." Ananias went and entered the house. He placed his hands on him and said, "Brother Saul, the Lord Jesus, who appeared to you on the road you were traveling, has sent me so that you may regain your sight and be filled with the Holy Spirit." At once something like scales fell from his eyes, and he regained his sight. Then he got up and was baptized. And after taking some food, he regained his strength. (Acts 9:3–19)

I don't know about you, but I find this to be a powerful testimony of what God is capable of doing. God is in the business of transforming people's lives. God is in the business of taking people who are living for this world and giving them a new identity in the person of Jesus. God is forming people for the kingdom, giving them new eyes to see that which matters most. Saul of Tarsus was on a mission to make followers of Jesus have the worst possible lives. He had no mercy and no remorse. Then Saul of Tarsus encountered the person of Jesus and everything changed. Jesus called him out of his depravity and made him into a new creation. He took the old Saul and gave him a new life. At one point, Saul was conforming to the things of this world, and after his encounter with Jesus, he began a new life of kingdom formation. The trajectory of his destination had changed. Saul was now homeward bound. On his way toward kingdom life, he offered his life to be used by God for the purpose and glory of God. Saul proclaimed the gospel of Jesus Christ on earth (Acts 9:20). This left people astonished, as they could not believe who it was that was proclaiming the good news of the gospel (Acts 9:21). Saul would later be known as the apostle Paul—and would be the author of many New Testament letters that we have today. God transformed this man. He put in him a heart and mind for the kingdom.

> God is in the business of taking people who are living for this world and giving them a new identity in the person of Jesus.

After encountering Jesus, it was evident that Paul was fully invested in kingdom formation. The world of Saul of Tarsus was polarizing and poisonous. Everything but Jesus was pulling for his attention. When Paul's eyes were open, he began to see things with kingdom lenses. Being conformed and transformed into the person who was after the heart of Jesus—Paul was all about kingdom formation.

KINGDOM FORMATION

After his conversion, the apostle Paul was someone who was on a perpetual mission to live with a kingdom mindset. He was homeward bound. And on this journey, he wrote letters to churches, giving them wisdom and insight into this journey as well. At one point, Paul was put in prison for preaching the gospel. While in prison, Paul wrote several letters to churches. One of those letters was intended for the church in Colossae. In this letter, you can see Paul's life narrative unfold. Paul wrote about what kingdom living looks like to the church in Colossae. He records this:

> So if you have been raised with Christ, seek the things above, where Christ is, seated at the right hand of God. Set your minds on things above, not on earthly things. For you died, and your life is hidden with Christ in God. When Christ, who is your life, appears, then you also will appear with him in glory. Therefore, put to death what belongs to your earthly nature: sexual immorality, impurity, lust, evil desire, and greed, which is idolatry. Because of these, God's wrath is coming upon the disobedient, and you once walked in these things when you were living in them. But now, put away all the following: anger, wrath, malice, slander, and filthy language from your mouth. Do not lie to one another, since you have put off the old self with its practices and have put on the new self. You are being renewed in knowledge according to the image of your Creator. In Christ there is not Greek and Jew, circumcision and uncircumcision, barbarian, Scythian, slave and free; but Christ is all and in all. (Col 3:1–11)

If we have been raised with Christ, we must seek the things above. This is where Paul grounds his audience. For many, seeking things above is a massive perspective shift. It is not easy to focus on things that are above or to be kingdom minded when everything around us is visible, experiential, and well, there. Our minds can be polluted by everything around us, which can lead us to forgo seeking the things that are above. Paul's remark here is to urge followers of Jesus in Colossae to live according to the instruction of Jesus to seek first the kingdom of God.³ Pursuing the person of Jesus will give followers of Jesus the ability to be kingdom minded. On our own strength, we are unable to achieve this mystery. But as we pursue Jesus more, he gives us the ability to seek first the kingdom of God.

So often, I hear Christians putting strenuous pressure on themselves to live up to the holy standard of God, or they strive to achieve and do more for Jesus. These are not bad ambitions except for the fact that these are impossible to attain without fully relying on Christ for help. We will exhaust ourselves in these endeavors. Regardless of how hard we try, we will never measure up. We will always fall short. Enter grace. Paul in his Letter to the Ephesians writes, "For you are saved by grace through faith, and this is not from yourselves; it is God's gift—not from works, so that no one can boast. For we are his workmanship, created in Christ Jesus for good works, which God prepared ahead of time for us to do" (Eph 2:8–10). Nothing we do can earn God's favor. God already decided to send his Son, Jesus Christ, to live a perfect life on earth as it is in heaven. He already came up with the solution for our sins. We don't need to find a solution for our sins; we need to find the one who resolves our sins. His name is Jesus. Followers of Jesus are not exempt from the gospel after they have received it once. Being a follower of Jesus means that we desperately yearn for the gospel daily. Each day, we need to die to ourselves, pick up our cross, and follow Jesus. Matthew records Jesus making this statement in his Gospel, "Jesus said to his disciples, "If anyone wants to follow after me, let him deny himself, take up his cross, and follow me. For whoever wants to save his life will lose it, but whoever loses his life because of me will find it. For what will it benefit someone if he gains the whole world yet loses his life? Or what will anyone give in exchange for his life?" (Matt 16:24–26). Being a people who seek first the kingdom of God—who are homeward bound—will cost us the pleasures of this world. We must not be infatuated with creation, but we must be infatuated with the Creator. When we can deny ourselves and seek first the kingdom of God, we will receive a strength that sets us free from the toil and labor of trying to be better followers of Jesus.

> *We don't need to find a solution for our sins; we need to find the one who resolves our sins.*

---

3. Barry et al., *Faithlife Study Bible*, Col 3:1.

What makes us devout followers of Jesus is that we are faithful and committed to our Savior. It's when we rely on Jesus to give us the ability to press on when we have nothing left to give. It's when we recognize that being a kingdom-minded person means that we must desperately desire Jesus to be our everything in life. And it is being continuously reminded that when we fall short of doing these things, the grace of Christ overshadows us. There are ways, however, that help us grow in our commitment and passion for Jesus. That is what chapter 2 is all about. But before we get there, I want to end this chapter by reminding us all that we are meant for something greater than this world has to offer. When we live with this mindset, we are living with a kingdom mindset. When we embrace this reality, we understand that we are here for just a moment, and then we go home. Kingdom formation simply means that we are being formed for life in the kingdom. To prepare for the kingdom, we must grow in our spiritual formation here on earth as it is in heaven. The garden of old is being restored.

GARDEN RESTORATION

We've addressed brokenness. We've addressed the beauty and pain of the garden. We've addressed the modern-day garden and what it means to chase after the wind. Now, we must look at hope. As followers of Jesus, everything ends with hope. Our hope is in an incredible God who saw that things were broken. Who saw that restoration and reconciliation were necessary. And this God provided a way for restoration to be possible. A broken and sin-ridden garden now has life. This life comes from the person of Jesus. We long to dwell with our good and gracious King Jesus when life here on earth is finished. Jesus is making all things new. He is bringing death to life. He is renewing hearts of stone and making them hearts of flesh. He is miraculously saving lost souls with the power of his love. Regardless of the situation, Jesus is making a new creation. Now, let us talk about what steps we can take to grow in our spiritual formation as we long to be kingdom people.

PROCESS AND REFLECT: HOMEWARD BOUND

1. What practical steps do you take to live for God each day?
2. What idols are preventing you from living a kingdom lifestyle?

3. How do you see the kingdom of God in everyday life?
4. What priorities do you have that overshadow kingdom growth in your life?
5. Have you had a Damascus Road experience when Jesus made himself known to you? Take some time to process that experience. What can you learn from your encounter with Jesus?

CHAPTER 2

Spiritual Vitality for Kingdom Life

We all, with unveiled faces, are looking as in a mirror at the glory of the Lord and are being transformed into the same image from glory to glory; this is from the Lord who is the Spirit.

—2 COR 3:18

WHEN I WAS IN high school, I was perhaps one of the scrawniest kids in school. I was six foot three and made of pure skin and bones. When it would get windy outside I would find myself starting to come up off the ground a little. I was a basketball player, and at times, being skin and bones was beneficial for me as I would be able to keep up with most people my height, demonstrating superb cardio. Other times, I found myself being crushed by people who were stronger than I was. I would get bumps and bruises from people who were pure tanks on the court. Toward the end of my senior year, I discovered a newfound passion for lifting weights. This passion began after I had lifted weights a few times and discovered actual muscle growth. I couldn't believe it at first, but I was eager to press on. The more I would work out, the more I would see results. After some years in the weight room, I began to feel more confident and just healthier as a person. Little did I know that working out had always been available to me. I had just never taken the next step to grow as an individual in this way.

Our physical self will eventually wear out. We can work hard at maintaining our physical bodies (which we absolutely should), but they will not last forever. We are spiritual beings. Our spiritual lives will last forever. We were destined for eternity, and eternity never ends. This means that the most important exercise that we can participate in is our spiritual formation. Being formed spiritually develops our souls and prepares us for kingdom life. This is done through our journey of growing in our walk with Jesus Christ, who is our Lord and Savior. He is who we must strive for. He is our source of everlasting life. He alone is the one who nourishes us and sustains our lives—forevermore. Jesus is our primary example of what a complete life looks like. Our spiritual vitality starts and ends with the person of Jesus. So if we are going to look more like Jesus here on earth, then let us take practical measures to grow in our relationship with him. Let us be conformed to the image of the Son of God (Rom 8:29) so that we can better represent the kingdom of God here on earth as it is in heaven.

SANCTIFICATION

When someone decides to follow Jesus, they immediately become a regenerated person. Their lives have been transformed by the power of the gospel. They have heard, received, and fully accepted the free gift of salvation that is offered in the person of Jesus. They have experienced regeneration. One of my favorite theologians, Millard Erickson, writes this on regeneration:

> Although regeneration is instantaneously complete, it is not an end in itself. As a change of spiritual impulses, regeneration is the beginning of a process of growth that continues throughout one's lifetime. The process of spiritual maturation is sanctification. Having noted that his readers were formerly dead but are now alive, Paul adds, "For we are God's handiwork, created in Christ Jesus to do good works, which God prepared in advance for us to do" (Eph 2:10). He speaks in Philippians 1:6 of continuing and completing what has been begun: "being confident of this, that he who began a good work in you will carry it on to completion until the day of Christ Jesus." The manifestations of this spiritual ripening are called the "fruit of the Spirit." They are the direct opposite of the work of the old nature, the flesh (Gal 5:19–23).[1]

Regeneration is what happens when we encounter our risen Lord Jesus. Who we were is no longer who we are. Everything changes. Our former self is swallowed up by the grace of God. We are no longer defined by the sin of this world and the sin that is in our hearts, but we are defined by the person

---

1. Erickson, *Christian Theology*, 874.

of Jesus. This is grace. This is regeneration. After we are regenerated, the formation process begins. This process is known as sanctification. As Erickson so eloquently puts it, Paul reminds the church in Philippi that the God who began a good work will carry it on to completion until the day of Christ Jesus (Phil 1:6). So we are saved into eternal fellowship with Jesus when we confess with our mouths that Jesus is Lord and believe in our hearts that God raised Jesus from the dead (Rom 10:9). After making this commitment, we then allow the Spirit of the living God to form us and mold us into the image of Jesus. This formation process will take a lifetime. Our spiritual vitality for kingdom life is demonstrated through the fruits of the Spirit. As we grow in the sanctification process, we will notice that the fruits of the Spirit begin to unfold in our daily lives. If we are growing toward kingdom life here on earth, then we will see growth in the areas of love, joy, peace, patience, kindness, goodness, faithfulness, gentleness, and self-control (Gal 5:22–23). We will unpack all of these for greater clarity.

> We are no longer defined by the sin of this world and the sin that is in our hearts, but we are defined by the person of Jesus.

Love

I won't spend too much time on this one, as a whole chapter is dedicated to what kingdom love looks like (ch. 3). Living out all of the fruits of the Spirit can be a challenge, but this one is a lot more challenging than it sounds. Love is not an easy action to demonstrate—especially in today's day and age. As division polarizes us at every angle, love falls farther and farther down the list of priorities in our lives. We simply choose not to love. It is easier not to love—especially our enemies. If we are going to grow in our spiritual vitality for kingdom life, love must be at the core of who we are. For one, Jesus gives us a perfect picture of love. "For God loved the world in this way: He gave his one and only Son, so that everyone who believes in him will not perish but have eternal life. For God did not send his Son into the world to condemn the world, but to save the world through him. Anyone who believes in him is not condemned, but anyone who does not believe is already condemned

> If we are going to grow in our spiritual vitality for kingdom life, love must be at the core of who we are.

because he has not believed in the name of the one and only Son of God" (John 3:16–18). The demonstration of love is on display through the person of Jesus. God gave Jesus Christ, his one and only Son, as a living sacrifice, to save humanity from sin and eternal death. That is massive. That is life changing. Our eternal security rests in the love that God had for us—by giving us Jesus Christ. Jesus paid the penalty for our sins on the Roman cross so that we may have life everlasting. This is love. Jesus says, "No one has greater love than this: to lay down his life for his friends" (John 15:13). The Greek word used here for "friends" is *philos* (φίλος), meaning a friend, an associate, a neighbor, and the like.[2] Jesus demonstrated this first and foremost by offering his life as a living sacrifice. He did this for the sake of saving the lives of those who are lost. He laid down his life so that we would live. This is love.

Would we lay down our lives for our brothers and sisters? Would we lay down our lives for our associates? Would we lay down our lives for our neighbors? What if our neighbors are our enemies—would we still lay down our lives for them? We naturally place conditions on our love toward others, whereas the love of God is unconditional. And if God's love was conditional, would we be lovable? It may be easy to see ourselves and other like-minded folks as lovable. But those who don't act like us, talk like us, think like us, live like us, believe like us, they are unlovable. If this is how we operate, then perhaps we need to encounter the fruit of love. Perhaps we have not fully grasped the love that God has for us. When we do, we will be forever changed. When we truly embrace the love of God for us, then we will learn to love our neighbors well. Sure, it will be challenging to love those who are different from us, but this is why we cannot depend on ourselves for that ability. Without Jesus, we're unable to love the unlovable. Let us cling to Jesus who alone is capable of giving us the strength to love others well.

Joy

Joy can be confusing. In my conversations, people often confuse joy with happiness. Happiness is circumstantial, whereas joy is eternal. The experience of happiness comes when we are in a moment and that moment begins to fill our hearts with a good spirit, and we can experience happiness

---

2. See https://www.blueletterbible.org/lexicon/g5384/csb/tr/0-1/.

in that moment. If conflict comes our way shortly after, it can be very easy to suppress that happiness. All of a sudden it can just disappear.

I experience bursts of happiness when I watch my favorite sports teams. I think about when I get home from church on Sundays in the fall and flip the TV on to the Chicago Bears game. The Bears score a touchdown and I am jumping out of my seat, filling the entire house with energy and loud noises. I am ecstatic when the Bears score a touchdown (because it doesn't happen often). I am standing, my heart is racing, and I could not be happier in the moment. Moments later, the opposing team finds their way back and scores a touchdown of their own. When this happens, you might as well not be around me. My mood shifts drastically. I was jumping out of my seat one moment, and the next, I was pouting. My happiness is gone. It is replaced with frustration and anger. This is what happiness looks like.

When it comes to joy, I am frequently reminded of one of the strangest passages in the Bible. The half-brother of Jesus, James, writes in his letter, "Consider it a great joy, my brothers and sisters, whenever you experience various trials" (Jas 1:2). At face value, this makes no sense at all. Why would somebody consider it a great joy when they face a trial in their life? Trials are challenging. And when we are talking about the wild roller coaster also known as our emotions, why would we ever consider our trials joy? Well, if we keep reading, we will get the answer. Why consider our trials great joy? James writes, "Because you know that the testing of your faith produces endurance. And let endurance have its full effect, so that you may be mature and complete, lacking nothing" (Jas 1:4–5). This is especially radical when we consider James's context. Jewish Christians were attempting to faithfully follow Jesus, and persecution broke out. This persecution caused followers of Jesus to disperse (Acts 8:1). Followers of Jesus were forced to leave their homes and spread out to the many gentile territories. This was uncomfortable. This was foreign. It was certainly far from ideal. Their faith was being tested, and their lives were on the line. These followers of Jesus were being purified in the fire. Their faith was being put to the test as persecution broke out. James's heart was that they would consider these trials that they were facing joy, because the trials would produce steadfastness and endurance in their faith. When we can find great joy in Jesus—even when things get hard—our faith grows. When our faith grows, we grow in the sanctification process. We begin to look more like a kingdom people. When we can't muster up joy in our circumstances, then it is the perfect time to start seeking the face of Jesus. When we do this, he will meet us exactly where we are and give us enough of himself for us to find joy. True joy comes from Jesus. Ask him for it. He will give it.

Peace

As you may be able to tell, none of these fruits are easily acquired. That is why we must depend on Christ to give us the ability to attain the fruits of the Spirit. Peace is no different. It is challenging to think that we can experience peace on this earth that is sin ridden and filled with hate, strife, anger, war, persecution, and chaos. How is it that we can experience peace when many things in this life don't make sense? Well, I'm glad you asked, because that is why we need Jesus. When I think of peace, I don't think of an emotion that gives me the feeling of serenity. When I think of peace, I think of the person of Jesus.

Every Christmas, I hear the same few verses about Jesus. It can easily get to the point where we take these verses for granted as some routine to go through. But if we take a pause and meditate on the true meaning of some of these verses, we will be blown away. One of the verses I hear and read every year is Isa 9:6. Isaiah writes, "For a child will be born for us, a son will be given to us, and the government will be on his shoulders. He will be named Wonderful Counselor, Mighty God, Eternal Father, Prince of Peace" (Isa 9:6). When Isaiah foretells the birth of Jesus, he offers some powerful statements on who Jesus will be. Jesus will be named Wonderful Counselor, Mighty God, Eternal Father, and Prince of Peace. Wow. Jesus, our risen Lord and Savior, is referred to as the *Prince of Peace*. J. Alec Motyer says this:

> In its highest use, "name" sums up character; it declares the person. The perfection of this King is seen in his qualification for ruling (*Wonderful Counsellor*), his person and power (*Mighty God*), his relationship to his subjects (*Everlasting Father*) and the society his rule creates (*Prince of Peace*).[3]

Here we see an incredible description of the person of Jesus. Isaiah demonstrates who Christ is and what his character reflects. Jesus is the Prince of Peace. When we allow Jesus to rule over our lives, we will be bearers of the

> *When we allow Jesus to rule over our lives, we will be bearers of the peace he gives.*

3. Motyer, *Isaiah*, 101.

peace he gives. Regardless of what we may be experiencing at the moment, we can be assured of the peace that is given to us in the person of Jesus. Because Jesus himself is peace. The peace that Jesus gives to us surpasses our human understanding (Phil 4:7). So possessing the peace of Christ simply means pursuing Jesus. Giving our time, energy, and effort over to the Prince of Peace will allow for our lives to experience a kingdom peace that we can live with for the rest of our lives. Enjoy this gift by enjoying Jesus.

Patience

As someone who lives in the US, I am aware of the pressures of instant gratification. I remember when I lived in Chicago, I discovered something called Amazon Prime Now. This service guarantees delivery to your house within two hours of your order. Two hours. You read that correctly. Talk about instant gratification. I wanted an item once, put an order in, and within two hours, sure enough, the package was sitting at my doorstep. What kind of world do we live in? But I was a fan. Because just like the rest of the country, I like to get everything fast.

The Christian life, more often than not, is the exact opposite of this. Instant gratification is far from how God works. God works in the waiting. It is in the waiting that we grow, are stretched, challenged, and sanctified. Endurance is a good thing in our faith, and often we find endurance in the waiting. Think about Abram. God made a promise to Abram that he would have land (Gen 12:1), numerous descendants (Gen 15:5), and a blessing for Abram and his descendants (Gen 22:17). This did not happen instantly. This was a process. There was a waiting period. Abram did not have the patience and took matters into his own hands (Gen 16–18). Eventually, God's promises to Abram were fulfilled (Gen 21). God was faithful. That is part of his character. God uses patience in our lives to create in us a dependence on him. The waiting period is not always enjoyable, but it is essential for our sanctification and spiritual formation. On our own, being patient is nearly impossible. This is why we need to trust and rely on Jesus to give us the ability to have supernatural patience that only he can give. When we possess the patience that only Jesus can offer, then we will be able to accept delay in our lives, knowing that it is meant to make us more like our Savior.

> *The waiting period is not always enjoyable, but it is essential for our sanctification and spiritual formation.*

Kindness

Kindness is a silly fruit of the Spirit to me. Let me explain. I first learned of kindness in my elementary school from my teacher. Mind I tell you that this was a secular elementary school. I learned how to be kind, and I tried. But, of course, life happens. Relationships are messy and broken. Hurt and pain exist. All of this can lead to not possessing this fruit of the Spirit. Later in my life I would become a Christian and learn of how kind and compassionate Jesus was. I knew this was the type of kindness that I wanted my life to portray. At face value, kindness is being friendly with others. Although kindness seems like a basic principle in life, it is not so easy to apply.

If we consider the state of our world, what we see is a major lack of kindness. Many are picking sides and fighting against each other. Everything is being politicized. Very little can be said without setting someone off and sending them into their bunker. This is seen in the church as much as it is seen outside of the church. This kind of lifestyle does not produce genuine kindness in the life of a kingdom person. It does the opposite. As kingdom people who are being formed into the image of Jesus, we are to be the front-runners in demonstrating kindness to a world that lacks it. When we consider the person of Jesus, we see what kindness truly looks like. Think about Zacchaeus. This was a man who was despised or overlooked by many because he was an unpleasant person. Barry J. Beitzel gives us a better picture of the person of Zacchaeus. Zacchaeus was a:

> Jewish chief publican who hired assistants to collect taxes at Jericho. He perhaps secured this position by purchasing the exclusive right to collect revenue in that region or by working as a subcontractor for another affluent official. In either case Zacchaeus himself accrued great wealth (largely by illegitimate means) from his customs enterprise at Jericho, a significant center of commerce, stationed along a major trade route connecting Jerusalem and its environs with the lands east of the Jordan.[4]

This man Zacchaeus was not someone who people wanted to be around. He was an illegitimate tax collector who duped people of their money. Uncle

---

4. Beitzel, "Zacchaeus."

Sam isn't a fan favorite nowadays either. Either way, from a human perspective, Zacchaeus was not someone who deserved to receive any sort of kindness. But per usual, leave it to Jesus to flip things upside down. The Gospel writer Luke records this in his Gospel:

> He entered Jericho and was passing through. There was a man named Zacchaeus who was a chief tax collector, and he was rich. He was trying to see who Jesus was, but he was not able because of the crowd, since he was a short man. So running ahead, he climbed up a sycamore tree to see Jesus, since he was about to pass that way. When Jesus came to the place, he looked up and said to him, "Zacchaeus, hurry and come down because today it is necessary for me to stay at your house." So he quickly came down and welcomed him joyfully. All who saw it began to complain, "He's gone to stay with a sinful man." But Zacchaeus stood there and said to the Lord, "Look, I'll give half of my possessions to the poor, Lord. And if I have extorted anything from anyone, I'll pay back four times as much." "Today salvation has come to this house," Jesus told him, "because he too is a son of Abraham. For the Son of Man has come to seek and to save the lost." (Luke 19:1–10)

Jews did not get along with tax collectors, as tax collectors worked for the Roman Empire.[5] Jews would consider them traitors. Think about that for a moment. A traitor is not someone we think of when we think of offering and extending kindness. Here we have a perfect example of Jesus flipping cultural norms upside down. Jesus is concerned about something far greater than seeing someone as a traitor. He sees an image-bearer. He sees someone who is made in the image of God and who needs to be loved, cared for, and allowed to know about a God who can save and offer everlasting life. That is Jesus's concern here. Jesus does not judge Zacchaeus for his past; Jesus offers him a future. A future that allows Zacchaeus to be a kingdom person.

What if we responded to our *enemies* the way that Jesus responded to Zacchaeus? What if instead of picking sides and fighting against each other, we chose to fight *for* each other? How much more would followers of Jesus display the kindness of Jesus if we modeled our lives after the way Jesus modeled his? Jesus's heart for Zacchaeus is a demonstration of kingdom kindness. This is the type of kindness that we must embody as people who long to live a life on earth as it is in heaven. This is a kindness that we can reflect on others as we grow deeper in our spiritual formation. As followers of Jesus, let us cling to Jesus as our source of kindness. When we do, we may be surprised at how we learn to treat others.

5. Barry et al., *Faithlife Study Bible*, Luke 19:2.

Goodness

Christmas is by far my favorite holiday to celebrate each year. Many things make Christmas great each year, but one of my favorite things about Christmas is the music. Playing the same old Christmas classics in the background all month long brings such familiarity during the season of Advent. Some people cannot stand Christmas music, and if that is you, I am praying for your heart as I write these words—there is still hope for you. But there is one particular Christmas song that always gets me thinking when I hear it. I'm sure you have heard of this song. It's called "Santa Claus Is Comin' to Town." There is a specific line in this song that strikes me every time I hear it. This is a song that talks about being good for the sake of goodness. This means that the entire purpose of being good is just for goodness itself. Well, that and, of course, being good so that Santa can put some extra presents underneath your Christmas tree. But I can understand the premise of this song when one is striving to be good for goodness' sake in terms of teaching morality. But as followers of Jesus, our call to *goodness* is far greater than merely practicing morality for morality's sake. We can never be good enough to the standard which God has called us to. We will perpetually fall short of God's standard of goodness, and our motivation to grow in our spiritual formation should never be spurred on by being good. Following Jesus means pursuing and committing oneself to trust that goodness has been achieved and accomplished on our behalf. Jesus alone can measure up to the standard of God's desired goodness. When we embody the fruit of the Spirit of goodness, we are choosing to embody Christ himself. Growth in goodness means growth in Christ. The challenge with this fruit of the Spirit is to press into the soul care that only Jesus can provide us with. He gently tends our souls with his mercy and grace. He constantly meets with us, and if we are receptive, he chisels away at our weary souls, making us more like him. He turns our ashes into beauty. And in Jesus, we are made good not for goodness' sake but for kingdom's sake.

Faithfulness

Faithfulness is a word of longevity. It intends a commitment until the very end. The struggle with faithfulness is that it is a major challenge to attain as sinful human beings. Instead of hanging on with longevity, there can be a tendency to sway from the many commitments in our lives. What about our commitment to the Lord? The question before us that causes us to reflect upon our hearts before God is this: Is our spiritual walk with the Lord filled with faithfulness and commitment to him, or do we find ourselves straying, not being able to find persistence and endurance in our faith journey? How we answer this question is very important. How we answer this question reveals our faithfulness to our Lord. Some may feel like they have a thriving relationship with our Lord. This is good. It is a sign of a healthy and growing spiritual vitality. Others may find themselves somewhere in the middle, growing in the Lord but also having bad days that may not involve the Lord. And then some may feel like the Lord is far and not present in their lives. The commitment levels of all of these categories are very different. One demonstrates a deep commitment to the Lord. One demonstrates an on-and-off commitment to the Lord. And one shows a depleting spiritual life that desperately needs the Lord to revive a drifting heart. This evaluation is not meant to shame or judge anyone. It is intended to cause one to reflect on their own spiritual journey, health, and vitality, all while seeking ways to connect with the Lord.

As we may find ourselves lacking in our faithfulness, there is one sure thing: God is faithful. He is faithful when we are not. God faithfully meets our needs and deeply cares for us. His faithfulness has no end. Jeremiah, the author of the book of Lamentations, wrote this: "Because of the Lord's faithful love we do not perish, for his mercies never end. They are new every morning; great is your faithfulness! I say, 'The Lord is my portion, therefore I will put my hope in him'" (Lam 3:22–24). Because of God's faithfulness to us, we can put all of our hope in him. Time after time, God proved himself faithful to his people. He was faithful in Abraham's life (Gen 12–22). God demonstrated his faithfulness to Moses in Exod 34 when he proclaimed:

> Because of God's faithfulness to us, we can put all of our hope in him.

> The Lord—the Lord is a compassionate and gracious God, slow to anger and abounding in faithful love and truth, maintaining faithful love to a thousand generations, forgiving iniquity, rebellion, and sin. But he will not leave the guilty unpunished, bringing the consequences of the fathers' iniquity on the children and grandchildren to the third and fourth generation. (Exod 34:6–7)

God, in his faithfulness, is both just and merciful. He is slow to anger and abounds in faithful love and truth. Israel's faithfulness to God fell short when they decided to bow down to a golden calf (Exod 32:4) instead of to

God himself. They were impatient. They were looking for a source of worship, and Moses was taking too long (Exod 32:1). Their faithfulness to God lacked longevity. When the test came, they proceeded to find satisfaction in a golden calf, rather than in God himself. Their faithfulness was scarce.

When we are a people who lack faithfulness, God in his never-changing character continues to be faithful. He does not give up on us. He persists in chasing after us even when we continue to run from him. Simply put, this is because God is faithful. Psalm 36 says, "Lord, your faithful love reaches to heaven, your faithfulness to the clouds" (Ps 36:5). What the psalmist intends to articulate here is the character of Yahweh. Yahweh's faithful love is covenantal. It is a bond between God and his people. It is not something that can be broken. God's faithful love never gives up on us. When we fall short, God fills in the gaps. He never leaves us high and dry. He is active in caring for us. No one is like our God. The prophet Micah had something to say about the faithfulness of God:

> Who is a God like you, forgiving iniquity and passing over rebellion for the remnant of his inheritance? He does not hold on to his anger forever because he delights in faithful love. He will again have compassion on us; he will vanquish our iniquities. You will cast all our sins into the depths of the sea. You will show loyalty to Jacob and faithful love to Abraham, as you swore to our ancestors from days long ago. (Mic 7:18–20)

Micah's hope was based on God's unchanging character.[6] He journeyed with God throughout his lifetime and was familiar with the character of God. God was loyal to those who came before Micah, and God was loyal to Micah. Micah reflected on the character of God that was displayed to those who came before him. God was loyal and faithful to Jacob and displayed faithful love to Abraham. Both Abraham and Jacob were part of leading the people of Israel. They were ministered to by God throughout their lives. God was faithful to them, even when they veered off track. He never failed them, nor did he neglect them. God was committed to them because of his faithfulness.

Faithfulness is a fruit of the Spirit. Faithfulness is part of our sanctification. When we are becoming more like Jesus, we are being formed into faithful people. Faithfulness is a trait of a kingdom person. Someone who is being formed into who they were meant to be. Someone who is being formed into who they ought to be—faithful. When we pursue Christ, he

---

6. Kevin Peacock, "Micah," in Blum and Wax, *CSB Study Bible*, 1418.

will form us into more faithful beings. Jesus alone will give us the ability to be faithful people. Possessing the image of Jesus means possessing his faithfulness. As we are formed into the image of Christ, we are actively growing in our faithfulness while being formed for the kingdom. The fruit of the Spirit known as faithfulness will flourish within our lives when we depend less on ourselves and more on the person of Jesus.

Gentleness

Brutal, prideful, arrogant, cruel, unpleasant. What if these words described who we were? My guess is that we would not be too fun to hang out with—at all. We can find ourselves defaulting to these character traits if we are not possessing the fruits of the Spirit in our lives. One of those fruits is *gentleness*. Being gentle can come across as a weakness, especially in an ever-polarizing world. We need to stand up for ourselves. Pick ourselves up by our bootstraps. Fight the fight. Prove to people why we're right and they're wrong. It's all about grit and making sure no one stomps on us. It's about having your fingers accessible to grab your cell phone at any moment, get on social media, and tear people down. We look for and find our tribes and draw near to those people. Everyone else is an enemy. This is how we are conditioned to think, act, and live. When everyone else is doing it, we might as well join right in and take a side. We spend more time being discipled by Fox News and CNN than Jesus Christ and his bride, the church. We are formed by the outside world, choosing to live in fear rather than resting in the wholehearted truth of who Jesus is. As we make the daily decision to listen to the voices of the world, we push the voice of the Holy Spirit away. All of this causes our spiritual formation to fade as we are formed by the things of this world. The more we are formed by the things of this world, the less we become a kingdom people. And if we are not seeking to become kingdom people, there will be an absence of gentleness in our lives. Gentleness is not a weakness; gentleness demonstrates the strength of Christ in us.

When referring to the person of Jesus, Dane Ortlund, in his excellent book *Gentle and Lowly*, writes this, "Meek. Humble. Gentle. Jesus is not trigger-happy. Not harsh, reactionary, easily exasperated. He is the most understanding person in the universe. The posture most natural to him is not a pointed finger but open arms."[7] Do yourself a favor and reread that quote

---

7. Ortlund, *Gentle and Lowly*, 19.

from Dane Ortlund. Read it again. Read it one more time. Jesus, God in the flesh (or God in a bod), is known for his meekness, humility, and gentleness. Ortlund's entire book is rooted in the passage found in Matt 11:28–29, where Jesus says, "Come to me, all of you who are weary and burdened, and I will give you rest. Take up my yoke and learn from me, because I am lowly and humble in heart, and you will find rest for your souls" (Matt 11:28–29). Jesus is so gentle with us. He is compassionate toward us. He is tender. When we are weary and burdened, Jesus calls us to himself, so that we can receive a rest that only he can give.

> When we are weary and burdened, Jesus calls us to himself, so that we can receive a rest that only he can give.

When arriving in Jerusalem on Palm Sunday, Jesus's triumphal entry was the fulfillment of a prophecy told in Zechariah. The Gospel writer Matthew records this of Zechariah's prophecy, "Tell Daughter Zion, 'See, your King is coming to you, gentle, and mounted on a donkey, and on a colt, the foal of a donkey'" (Matt 21:5). You read that correctly—the King of kings and Lord of lords entered the gates of Jerusalem on a donkey. Zechariah prophesied that this king would come to Jerusalem, *gentle*, mounted on a donkey. When I think of kings or rulers, I don't think of them as being gentle. I think of King Herod and how he ruled and displayed his authority. Here is a glimpse of what King Herod was like:

> Herod was a strange mix of a clever and efficient ruler and a cruel tyrant. On the one hand, he was distrustful, jealous, and brutal, ruthlessly crushing any potential opposition. The Jews never accepted him as their legitimate king, and this infuriated him. He constantly feared conspiracy. He executed his wife when he suspected she was plotting against him. Three of his sons, another wife, and his mother-in-law met the same fate when they too were suspected of conspiracy. Herod, trying to be a legitimate Jew, would not eat pork, but he freely murdered his sons! Matthew's account of Herod's slaughter of the infants in Bethlehem fits well with what we know of the king's ambition, paranoia, and cruelty (Matt 2:1–18).[8]

Here we see one of the worst kings that ruled the earth. Not all kings were like this, but most of them would rule with a desire to be power hungry and were filled with corruption. David was another king in the Bible. Many

---

8. "What Herod Was Like," in Zondervan Academic, "Who Was Herod?"

believe that David was the best version of a king in the time of Scripture, but even still, David was far from perfect. David made many errors and mistakes. David murdered and committed adultery. He would frequently sin but would quickly realize that repentance was needed. One of David's most famous psalms was his psalm of repentance, Ps 51. Solomon was a great king as well. But Solomon, too, found himself dealing with a plethora of issues (see 1 Kgs 11).

When we consider King Jesus, we see a humble King who was always putting the needs of others before his own. Jesus's power as a King was demonstrated in his gentleness. He was unlike any other king. To be a gentle king seems like an oxymoron. But this is who Jesus was. This is who Jesus still is. He is a gentle King who desires that we would come to him. Dane Ortlund, once again, does a sensational job of encapsulating the gentleness of Jesus:

> Look to Christ. He deals gently with you. It's the only way he knows how to be. He is the high priest to end all high priests. As long as you fix your attention on your sin, you will fail to see how you can be safe. But as long as you look to this high priest, you will fail to see how you can be in danger. Looking inside ourselves, we can anticipate only harshness from heaven. Looking out to Christ, we can anticipate only gentleness.[9]

We have an approachable King. We have a King who deals gently with us. We have a King who is tenderhearted and cares about every little detail in our lives. He is meek and humble. He is faithful and trustworthy. He is constant and consistent. The Savior of this crazy world we live in wants to know us personally. He meets us in the hills and valleys of life and offers us his gentleness and care. He weeps and mourns with us. He celebrates and rejoices with us. He is personal, kind, and compassionate. This is our God and our King. This is the Ruler of our lives and our hearts. Search for him. Seek him. Find him. Jesus nourishes our souls with his gentleness. Let us receive the gentleness of Christ and reciprocate this posture to those around us.

Self-Control

We have reached the final fruit of the Spirit as we see it in Gal 5. This fruit of the Spirit is known as *self-control*. I am not a big fan of grocery shopping.

---

9. Ortlund, *Gentle and Lowly*, 57.

But just because I am not a fan of something does not mean I still don't do it. When I go grocery shopping with my wife, it can be both a blessing and a curse. The blessing is that my wife and I get to spend time together. The curse is that when you take a hungry man to the grocery store, you will certainly spend way more money than originally intended. My wife has a list and an agenda of all that is needed, but I look at all of the things that I want. I especially struggle when it comes to all of the steak options. I typically try to convince my wife that we must have steak at the house. She is usually gracious toward my request. But it doesn't stop with the steak. I continue our grocery shopping endeavor imagining all of the snacks I could be eating once we get home. I find myself filling the grocery cart with all sorts of things that are unnecessary—often getting a look from my wife. Don't worry, I deserve it. We spend way too much money when I go, and when we get home, many of the snacks I get I may not even eat. I lack self-control when we go grocery shopping.

Self-control is a fruit of the Spirit—yet many of us lack this fruit. Just as the first man and woman lacked self-control in the garden of Eden—partaking of the fruit of the tree of the knowledge of good and evil—we, too, can find ourselves struggling with this fruit of the Spirit. In moments when we need to tame the tongue, we may be tempted to blurt out harsh things toward someone. James writes in his letter to the dispersed Jews, "With the tongue we bless our Lord and Father, and with it we curse people who are made in God's likeness. Blessing and cursing come out of the same mouth. My brothers and sisters, these things should not be this way" (Jas 3:9–10). When we lack the self-control needed to tame our tongues, we show that we need work in this area of our spiritual formation. Every one of us has said something to someone that we may not have meant, but that does not excuse how we are to talk to people and talk about people. Gossip is a common symptom of a lack of self-control. Many Christians will strive to be more like Christ, but when it comes to gossip—hot, feisty news or information about someone—there can be a tendency to talk. With the same mouth that Jesus is worshiped, others are blasted. Even in a day where everything in the world is made political, followers of Jesus look less like followers of Jesus and more like the camps they associate themselves with. Lacking self-control, especially with the tongue, can be a deceitful and poor way to display kingdom life. We are called to higher standards than this. Yes, we will fail. Yes, we will let people down. This is why the grace of God is so incredibly rich. But we need to strive after the person of Jesus and seek authentic kingdom formation so that we may look more like Christ and less like the world.

Self-control is lacking not only in the tongue, but it can also be lacking in all of life. This can be impulsive behavior. An outburst of emotions. Being so angry and fired up that we cannot think straight. We may be impatient, impulsive, or easily irritated due to a lack of self-control. All of these things are normal, but they are not the end goal. They are not a product of sanctification for kingdom formation. When we are truly committed to becoming kingdom people, God can do extraordinary things in our lives. He can set us free from the bondage of the things that hold us back. God in his faithfulness is capable of giving us the self-control we need in our lives through the power of the Holy Spirit. When we rely less on ourselves and more on Jesus, we will truly experience transformative power in our lack of self-control. God made us in his image. Sin distorted that image. God, in his sovereign grace, gives us the ability, strength, and power needed to overcome anything that we lack. He can restore our self-control and give us all that we need to maintain it. Lean in. Ask. Trust in a God who is able. When you do, watch for the miraculous work that he can do.

FRUITS OF THE SPIRIT FOR SPIRITUAL FORMATION

We spent time looking at all nine fruits of the Spirit. These fruits help us identify our strengths and weaknesses when it comes to our spiritual growth and formation. When we are living our lives with a kingdom mindset, the fruits of the Spirit will naturally begin to take form in our lives. The hope is that throughout our journey of following Jesus, we will possess these fruits more and more. Our spiritual vitality must be nourished by the blood of Jesus so that we may experience life on earth as it is in heaven. On our own, we will never achieve the fruits of the Spirit. It is by the grace of God in Christ alone that we will grow deeper in our spiritual journey. Cling to Jesus, and allow him to form you into who you were created to be.

BEING SATISFIED IN CHRIST

Another element of our spiritual vitality for kingdom life is learning to be satisfied only in Christ Jesus. When my family moved to central Wisconsin, we embarked upon a new and fresh journey that God had in store for us. When we arrived, there was much to get used to. Going from a big city to a smaller town was a big change. Through it all, we knew this was where God had us. As we were familiarizing ourselves with our new environment, we discovered shops, stores, and town favorites all around. But there was one place in particular that once we visited, our lives were transformed. This place was a local dairy that offered the best soft-serve ice cream one could ever desire (no, I'm not just saying that). This was quite possibly the best ice cream I had ever consumed. Everything made sense—God brought us here because he did not want my family to miss out on something so good—something that had a foretaste of eternity. Okay, maybe I am overreacting (just a bit), but this was certainly the kind of experience that you wanted to never go away. It was both fulfilling and satisfying. The problem, however, is that I don't do too well with dairy. This means this fulfilling and satisfying experience did not last, nor did it feel good after the fact. It kind of left me in a place which I wish I never got to. The satisfaction that I was experiencing at the dairy quickly disappeared and left me disappointed and uneasy.

There are many things in this world that beg for our attention. It is inevitable to look around and attempt to find fulfillment and satisfaction in what the world may offer. The truth is, there are plenty of things that can satisfy us here on earth. They are everywhere. Whether it be new technology, food, clothing, a new car, a new house, or fill-in-your-blank, eventually, that honeymoon period dwindles. We are left unfulfilled, displeased, and oftentimes dissatisfied with the product we consume. There is always a longing for fulfillment and satisfaction, but why does it feel like even the best of things wear off? This is because the world we live in is temporary. Everything we do is temporary. It is only for a season. Our lives are also temporary. We come into this world, live, and leave this world. We were certainly meant for something greater than temporary, worldly pleasures.

I am here to tell you (and myself) that there is only one source of everlasting fulfillment and satisfaction. That fulfillment and satisfaction is in Christ Jesus. Our souls are in a perpetual state of longing. We are longing to be fulfilled and satisfied. When we receive Jesus Christ, our Lord and Savior, while treasuring him as our everything, he will provide for us an ultimate source of satisfaction. He will fulfill our every longing. He will never lead us to feel empty or void. Jesus can and does offer us everlasting satisfaction. Have you given him a chance to quench your thirst? Have you allowed Jesus to do mighty work in your life? If you have, I hope that you are reminded of the goodness of Jesus in your life. If you have not given Jesus a chance yet, I encourage you to consider giving your life to Jesus, while allowing Jesus to change your life. He will radically transform you from the inside out. Let the Spirit of the living God lead you and guide you so that your soul may be satisfied. Take a deep breath and breathe in the goodness of God. The grace of God is upon you—offering you the satisfaction that can be found only in the gospel. May your soul thirst for Jesus. May you be satisfied in the gospel. May you be fulfilled by the everlasting promises of who God is and what he has done for you.

FORMED FOR THE KINGDOM

We've looked at regeneration—the fact that we are made into a new creation right after giving our lives to Jesus at conversion. We looked at the process of becoming more like Christ (sanctification) by obtaining the fruits of the Spirit in our lives. We dug deeper into each fruit of the Spirit and hopefully understood that none of the fruits of the Spirit are attainable apart from the grace of Christ. Christ alone is our help. He alone gives us the ability to obtain the fruits of the Spirit. So when we give ourselves over to Jesus, we become more like Jesus. When we try to form ourselves, we will fall short, time and time again. We are not responsible for making ourselves *better Christians*. We are responsible for faithfully following Jesus every day of our lives, and he will transform us into kingdom people. When we are being formed into kingdom people, we will find absolute satisfaction in Jesus. He alone will satisfy us and our every need.

PROCESS AND REFLECT: SPIRITUAL VITALITY FOR KINGDOM LIFE

1. Which fruit of the Spirit is most prevalent in your life? What has caused this to be the case?
2. Which fruit of the Spirit do you need to work on the most? What steps do you need to take to get there?
3. How can depending on Jesus enable you to grow in the fruits of the Spirit?

PART TWO: A Kingdom Lifestyle

CHAPTER 3

Kingdom Love

For God so loved the world that he gave his one and only Son, that whoever believes in him shall not perish but have eternal life. For God did not send his Son into the world to condemn the world, but to save the world through him.

—JOHN 3:16–17

IN THE FALL OF 2022, my wife and I went to visit family in Brooklyn, New York. It was an enjoyable trip with many memories and lots of experiences with delicious food. When we were coming back from our trip, we got stuck at Newark Liberty International Airport due to a flight delay. We waited and waited. Finally, at about eleven at night, we were told that our airplane was ready for us. We boarded the plane—exhausted. Since we live in a small town in rural Wisconsin, the closest larger airport that we could fly into was the Minneapolis–Saint Paul International Airport, where we had left our car before the trip. It was about one in the morning at this time and we were ready to be home. Both tired and exhausted, I felt like it would be a good idea to push the speed limit so that we could get home faster. I was comfortably going approximately twenty-five to thirty miles over the speed limit. The drive was going great until an hour in. As I was casually speeding, I began to notice a red-and-blue ambiance in my rearview mirror. I slammed my brakes and hoped that I was not going to get pulled over for taking advantage of the speed limit. It was too late. The police officer was getting closer and closer until it was obvious—I got caught. I had a bad feeling about going fast, but I had kept pushing my limits. I received a ticket for a price I am not happy to admit. The entire way home after being pulled over, I thought to myself—what was I thinking?

THE POWER OF GRACE

There is a story in the Gospel of John that is thematically similar to what I experienced. The outcome, however, was completely different.

> At dawn he [Jesus] went to the temple again, and all the people were coming to him. He sat down and began to teach them. Then the scribes and the Pharisees brought a woman caught in adultery, making her stand in the center. "Teacher," they said to him, "this woman was caught in the act of committing adultery. In the law Moses commanded us to stone such women. So what do you say?" They asked this to trap him, in order that they might have evidence to accuse him. Jesus stooped down and started writing on the ground with his finger. When they persisted in questioning him, he stood up and said to them, "The one without sin among you should be the first to throw a stone at her." Then he stooped down again and continued writing on the ground. When they heard this, they left one by one, starting with the older men. Only he was left, with the woman in the center. When Jesus stood up, he said to her, "Woman, where are they? Has no one condemned you?" "No one, Lord," she answered. "Neither do I condemn you," said Jesus. "Go, and from now on do not sin anymore." (John 8:2–11)

Here we have a woman who was caught in adultery. While Jesus was teaching, a handful of scribes and Pharisees brought this adulterous woman into the presence of Jesus, so that she might receive a fair and just consequence for her actions. It is important to note who the woman caught in adultery was dealing with. D. A. Carson writes, "The scribes were the recognized students and expositors of the law of Moses, but so central was the law in the life and thought of first-century Palestinian Jews that the scribes came to assume something of the roles of lawyer, ethicist, theologian, catechist, and jurist. Most of them, but certainly not all, were Pharisees by conviction."[1] This group of people who were considered to be the religious elite of their day arrived before Jesus and presented a woman caught in adultery for her

---

1. Carson, *Gospel According to John*, 334.

wrongful actions. Even though the woman was caught in this act, she was also being sinned against by the man involved. He may or may not have been taken as well, that we do not know, but we cannot excuse his behavior either. Was there mutual consent? Was she forced into the act? Either way, the man sinned as much as the woman sinned during this act of adultery. The woman happened to be the one who was caught by the religious leaders and brought to Jesus. One would think that Jesus would abide by the law and give the order to the scribes and Pharisees to proceed with stoning the woman for her wrongful action. Instead, what Jesus displayed was a heart of grace and love toward the woman. The outcome of her action was not what was expected. Jesus's response was unexpected. He said to the scribes and Pharisees, "The one without sin among you should be the first to throw a stone at her" (John 8:7). How did the scribes and Pharisees respond to Jesus? They left. One by one. They, too, realized that they had sin in their lives that was not dealt with. As they departed, Jesus remained with the woman. Jesus reiterated that he did not condemn the woman for her actions. He forgave her. She was given a fresh start. His love for her was greater than her sin. The woman's sin did not define who she was. Jesus defined who she was. Jesus demonstrated what kingdom love looks like to the woman caught in adultery.

When we consider the weight of Jesus's response to the woman caught in adultery, we must do our best to comprehend this kind of love. It is certainly a love that the woman did not deserve. According to the law, she was meant to be stoned to death for her actions. But Jesus offers a love that is greater than we can imagine. It is a love that looks nothing like the love that we know or understand. The love Jesus offers is unconditional. It goes beyond our comprehension. This is the beauty of who Jesus is because Jesus himself is love. The unconditional love of Jesus redefines the conditional love we are prone to live with. When we understand and embody this kind of love, we truly begin to represent kingdom love.

Our sin is heavy. Our sin is burdensome. Our savior is gracious and kind. The love that Jesus offered the woman caught in adultery is the same love that he offers to us. When we feel like we have gotten to the point where our sin is unbearable, our Savior waits for us to come to him. When we come to Jesus in repentance, he wraps us in his loving arms as he forgives us and delivers us from the weight of our sins. We are forgiven. Our sin no longer defines who we are. We are made new in Jesus because of his love for us.

THE PRODIGAL

I grew up in the church. It was a traditional, conservative Baptist church. I would often feel judged for my every action. Whenever I would do something wrong (which was often), I would feel shame, because that was what was being taught to me. I felt like God did not love me and did not care about me. I got to the point in my journey with religion where I no longer wanted to be part of it. When I got older, I was eager to leave the church and explore the things of this world. I got into the party scene and sought worldly pleasures over the pleasures of following Jesus. I left the church I grew up in and began to live a double life. I would go to church once in a while, but the party scene awaited me with arms wide open. I traded away my religion for the world and was certainly enjoying my life. That is, until I hit rock bottom. One night after a long night of partying, I felt broken and defeated. I felt like I no longer wanted to live the party life but was struggling to leave. I was desperate to find hope in my life that felt hopeless. I remember praying that night and telling God that if he was real to show up and take away this lifestyle that I was participating in. That night I had a dream of light and darkness fighting for me. I woke up in the morning thinking, was God trying to send me a message? I felt the pull—the pull of the Holy Spirit—at that moment. There was an old Bible that sat on a nightstand at my parents' home. I felt compelled to open it up and read it. I flipped through it until I reached the New Testament book of Matthew. That night, I read the entire book. In my reading, I was able to meet and encounter Jesus. It was an encounter unlike anything I had experienced before. Jesus gave his life for me, so that night, I decided to give my life to Jesus. I confessed my sin-filled life and received the forgiveness of my Savior. From that moment on, everything changed. I had been lost, but now I was found. A prodigal had returned.

LOVING THE PRODIGAL

Some of us have experienced a life committed to knowing and following Jesus. Others did not grow up in the church and came to find Jesus later in life. Some grew up in the church and ran off—only to discover that life without Jesus is a life without hope and purpose. The latter was my personal experience. When I met Jesus, I discovered his love for me. Regardless of how far I had drifted, I was able to return to where I was meant to be—the arms of God.

Jesus tells a parable in the book of Luke that demonstrates the unconditional love of God. Luke writes:

> He also said, "A man had two sons. The younger of them said to his father, 'Father, give me the share of the estate I have coming to me.' So he distributed the assets to them. Not many days later, the younger son gathered together all he had and traveled to a distant country, where he squandered his estate in foolish living. After he had spent everything, a severe famine struck that country, and he had nothing. Then he went to work for one of the citizens of that country, who sent him into his fields to feed pigs. He longed to eat his fill from the pods that the pigs were eating, but no one would give him anything. When he came to his senses, he said, 'How many of my father's hired workers have more than enough food, and here I am dying of hunger! I'll get up, go to my father, and say to him, "Father, I have sinned against heaven and in your sight. I'm no longer worthy to be called your son. Make me like one of your hired workers."' So he got up and went to his father. But while the son was still a long way off, his father saw him and was filled with compassion. He ran, threw his arms around his neck, and kissed him. The son said to him, 'Father, I have sinned against heaven and in your sight. I'm no longer worthy to be called your son.' "But the father told his servants, 'Quick! Bring out the best robe and put it on him; put a ring on his finger and sandals on his feet. Then bring the fattened calf and slaughter it, and let's celebrate with a feast, because this son of mine was dead and is alive again; he was lost and is found!' So they began to celebrate. "Now his older son was in the field; as he came near the house, he heard music and dancing. So he summoned one of the servants, questioning what these things meant. 'Your brother is here,' he told him, 'and your father has slaughtered the fattened calf because he has him back safe and sound.' Then he became angry and didn't want to go in. So his father came out and pleaded with him. But he replied to his father, 'Look, I have been slaving many years for you, and I have never disobeyed your orders, yet you never gave me a goat so that I could celebrate with my friends. But when this son of yours came, who has devoured your assets with prostitutes, you slaughtered the fattened calf for him.' 'Son,' he said to him, 'you are always with me, and everything I have is yours. But we had to celebrate and rejoice, because this brother of yours was dead and is alive again; he was lost and is found.'" (Luke 15:11–32)

Here we see three characters in a story that is vital to understanding the love of God. Jesus gives three parables in Luke 15 to sinners and tax collectors, ending with the longest parable of the three—the parable of the prodigal son. In this story, we see two sons. One who followed his father's rules and one who took his father's inheritance to go and live the life he wanted to live. The life chosen by the younger son was reckless and wicked. The lifestyle chosen by the younger son was selfish. He wanted to live for all of the pleasures the world had to offer. After some time, this caught up with him. He realized that the life he had chosen was starting to catch up with him. He wanted to return to his father. Upon his return, the younger son saw his father at a distance. The father had compassion for his wayward son (Luke 15:20). When his son came to him, the father wrapped his arms around him and embraced him. The father requested the best robe and the fattened calf to be given to his son, because he once had been lost and now he was found.

THE YOUNGER SON

A wayward son that once was lost and now is found. He tried to live a life that elevated himself and neglected God's best for him. He drifted away for a season of his life and realized that he was not living the life he was called to live. He came back to the father, and the father's arms were open wide. His reckless living was forgiven and forgotten. The father was filled with love and compassion for his wayward son. He welcomed him back into the family.

Some of us relate to the wayward son in this story. We have lived lives that squandered the goodness that God has provided for us. We knew what was best for us, but we decided to take matters into our own hands. In this endeavor, we lived recklessly and watched everything fall apart before our very eyes. We needed to stop what we were doing and make a complete 180 in our lives. We decided that we would release the wickedness in our lives—with the help of God—and run back into his loving arms. When we did, God met us there with compassion and embraced us into his presence.

This may be part of your story. Perhaps you are still in a place where you feel wayward and far from God. Regardless of where you are at, know that God is waiting for you to return home. His arms are open wide, and his compassion toward you is full. Your past does not define you. You are defined by the person and work of Jesus Christ. Release your burdens upon his shoulders. He will take them, carry them for you, and set you free from them. On your own, you will not be able to make it through too far. So give God your absolute dependence, and he will give you rest. Your past is recreated into who God intended you to be. Confess your sin, come to him, and live in the goodness that can be found only in the person of Jesus. Embrace his compassion and love for you.

THE OLDER SON

When we read the parable of the prodigal son, we often just focus on the younger son. But there is so much to learn from the older son in the parable that Jesus told. When studying the older son, it is apparent that he represents the religious leaders (scribes and Pharisees). Instead of rejoicing at the return of his younger, wayward brother, the older brother was angry and upset that his father would throw a feast for the younger brother after all that he had done (Luke 15:28–30). One commentator puts it this way: "Pharisees, and perhaps other Jews who considered themselves righteous [,] . . . were bothered by the warm welcome that Jesus gave to those they classified as sinners."[2] Since this story represents and reflects the love the father has for his people—especially those who are lost—the older brother's frustration represents the frustration that scribes and Pharisees had with the way Jesus cared for sinners and those who were far from God. The parable of the prodigal son is the third in a series of parables that talks about something being lost and then being found.

Jesus's heart in the triad of parables in Luke 15 demonstrates that God does not give up on those who are lost or far from him. God doesn't give up on those who are far from him, because he loves and cares deeply for his image-bearers. He desires that relationships will be restored. He desires that the wayward would come to him so that they, too, will have a seat at the table of glory. This, of course, bothered the older brother. He was frustrated. He became jealous and envious of the father's treatment of the younger son. We could understand the older brother as being someone who is living a life of legalism: I did all the right things. I said all the right words. I behaved well. My family is in order. My kids are perfect and obedient. My household is glamorous. But I get angry when people don't live like I do. I get frustrated when people don't look like me or act like me. It is not about what we do or don't do that earns God's favor and love. It is about having a heart of desperation and longing to be in his presence, recognizing that we are not good enough and Jesus is. The younger brother recognized his need to be in the father's house; the older brother stood there and pouted.

Let us not be a people who pride ourselves in our Christian achievements and accomplishments—rather, let us humbly offer ourselves to the

---

2. Barry et al., *Faithlife Study Bible*, Luke 15:29.

Lord, fully dependent and repentant. Let us be reminded that God loves us so dearly that he is willing to do whatever it takes to chase after us. Let us not measure our religiosity and compare it to others, while neglecting our own need to simply be in the presence of God. We are all a work in progress, and there is humility in that. Run to the father whose arms are open wide, and know that his gracious love is waiting to embrace your precious life.

THE LOVING FATHER

We have looked at two out of the three characters in the parable of the prodigal son. Now we shift gears and focus on the father. Right from the get-go of this story, the father is confronted by his younger son. The request made by his son was truly insulting. The younger son said, "Father, give me the share of the estate I have coming to me" (Luke 15:12). This language here, stating "share of the estate *I have coming to me,*" implies that the son is ready for the father to no longer exist, because to demand a portion of the estate, means the father must no longer be around. The younger son has no care in the world for the father's existence—rather, he just wants to reap the material benefits that the father may provide. Imagine being the father in this situation. You would be taken through an emotional roller coaster as your child simply wants the benefits of having you as their parent but no relationship. This is not uncommon in our world. Many parents can relate to the pain of the father in this story. Perhaps a child is wayward and has completely left the family. Perhaps a child lost a parent and has never felt close or connected to them. These are all real and painful situations. Regardless of one's experience with their biological family—rest assured that the family of God is different. As we see in this story, the father desires only that his son would return. The father wants to be reunited with his wayward son and simply wants his son back in his presence. When our earthly families fail us—whatever that looks like for each one of us—our heavenly father never fails us. His faithful love endures forever. God's love is eternal. Our understanding of love does not compare to the love that we can find in God. The love that God offers is unconditional. It is a kingdom love. Psalm 136 is a beautifully written psalm that highlights God's track record with a phrase about his faithfulness. Then, it is followed by the statement "His faithful love endures forever." The psalmist writes:

> Give thanks to the Lord, for he is good. His faithful love endures forever.
> Give thanks to the God of gods. His faithful love endures forever.

> Give thanks to the Lord of lords. His faithful love endures forever.
> He alone does great wonders. His faithful love endures forever.
> He made the heavens skillfully. His faithful love endures forever.
> He spread the land on the waters. His faithful love endures forever.
> He made the great lights: His faithful love endures forever.
> The sun to rule by day, His faithful love endures forever.
> The moon and stars to rule by night. His faithful love endures forever.
> He struck the firstborn of the Egyptians His faithful love endures forever.
> And brought Israel out from among them. His faithful love endures forever.
> With a strong hand and outstretched arm. His faithful love endures forever.
> He divided the Red Sea. His faithful love endures forever.
> And led Israel through, His faithful love endures forever.
> But hurled Pharaoh and his army into the Red Sea. His faithful love endures forever.
> He led his people in the wilderness. His faithful love endures forever.
> He struck down great kings. His faithful love endures forever.
> And slaughtered famous kings—His faithful love endures forever.
> Sihon king of the Amorites. His faithful love endures forever.
> And Og king of Bashan—His faithful love endures forever.
> And gave their land as an inheritance, His faithful love endures forever.
> An inheritance to Israel his servant. His faithful love endures forever.
> He remembered us in our humiliation. His faithful love endures forever.
> And rescued us from our foes. His faithful love endures forever.
> He gives food to every creature. His faithful love endures forever.
> Give thanks to the God of heaven! His faithful love endures forever.

This is the God who is after our very heart. He has done great things and continues to do great things. This is God's reputation. He is faithful, and his faithful love endures forever. Even still, we tend to run.

If we think about our own lives—how often do we treat God the way the younger son treated the father? God, I need you to give me my share, and I am going to run off, leaving you behind. I am going to make my own choices, my own decisions, even if it harms you and me. When I consider my journey, I know that I have treated God this way. I still make selfish decisions that allow me to experience what I want, even if that means I put God on the back burner. In those moments God patiently waits for my return. His arms are open wide. God desires that I would run

> When we choose to abandon God for selfish gain, God longs for our arrival back into his loving presence.

into his loving arms and be embraced by him. When we choose to abandon God for selfish gain, God longs for our arrival back into his loving presence. Our choice to abandon God only urges God to pursue us more. God is willing to recover what is lost regardless of the cost. He never quits on us. This is the love of the father. The love that is offered to us by God is a love that we cannot comprehend.

RECEIVING GOD'S LOVE AND OFFERING IT TO OTHERS

I am not a big fan of cardio. I used to run well back in middle school and high school. I played basketball and was in pretty decent shape. Nowadays, cardio is one of my enemies. We don't have a great relationship. My wife and I traveled to Asheville, North Carolina, to celebrate our anniversary as well as my graduation from my doctoral work. While we were in the mountains of Asheville, we made the decision that we would go on a hike. I will let you decide who made that decision. Let's just say I wasn't crazy about hiking, but I decided to suck it up and just go. So we went. As we began our hike, I was feeling pretty confident. Things were going well, and I was full of energy and adrenaline. Shortly into our hike, I noticed a sign. As I got closer, I could not believe my eyes. The sign I was confronted with read, "This is Bear Country." All of a sudden, I began to experience butterflies in my stomach. I began to look over my shoulder every few steps as I was fearing for my life. The trail we were on was gradually increasing in difficulty with several elevations. I kept wanting to turn around and just go back to our cabin in the woods. But that was unrealistic. So I kept pressing on. My lack of cardiovascular strength began to show. The challenge before me became more and more complex.

One of the most complex challenges in our lives as followers of Jesus is loving people the way God loves them. We have looked at just a few examples of God's unconditional love for his creatures. The love that God has for us is unexplainable. His love is persistent and consistent. What if we were able to embody this kind of love from the Creator of love? What would our lives look like if we were defined by the way we loved God and others?

According to Jewish tradition, the Torah consists of 613 laws. These laws could have been summed up in the Ten Commandments that God gave to Moses (Exod 20:2–17). Having this history as our context, let's fast forward to Matthew's Gospel. Jesus was confronted by an expert of the law

Kingdom Love

(Matt 22:35). During this confrontation, the expert of the law sought to test Jesus. Jesus was asked which command in the law is the greatest (Matt 22:36). His response was revolutionary:

> He said to him, "Love the Lord your God with all your heart, with all your soul, and with all your mind. This is the greatest and most important command. The second is like it: Love your neighbor as yourself. All the Law and the Prophets depend on these two commands." (Matt 22:37–40)

Loving God with all of our heart, soul, and mind, and loving others as ourselves, is essential to living out the commands of God. These two commands demonstrate the authentic heart of an individual. God offers us his sacred love. It is a love that we don't deserve and sometimes may not even understand. Nonetheless, it is freely given to us. For some, it is easy to receive. For others, it is unfathomable. Either way, this love is given to us through the person of Jesus Christ. The Gospel writer John writes, "For God so loved the world that he gave his one and only Son, that whoever believes in him shall not perish but have eternal life. For God did not send his Son into the world to condemn the world, but to save the world through him" (John 3:16–18). The eternal life that is offered by Jesus exists because of God's love for us. Putting our faith and trust in Jesus allows us to receive life everlasting. We can love because God showed us how to love first (1 John 4:19). When we find it to be a challenge to love others well, we ought not to rely on our own understanding of how we ought to love—rather, we are to lean on Jesus to give us the ability to love the unlovable. It will always be a challenge to love others—especially those who are very different from us—but that is not an excuse to not love people. Let us be reminded that God is constant and always pursues us with his love. God alone is capable of giving us the ability to love others as ourselves. This is not something that we can do on our own. In our natural form, we are love-violating sinners who are desperate for a Savior to show us how to love well. Praise be to God that we do indeed have a Savior who has brought us into his loving, eternal family by his love. This is kingdom love.

> *When we find it a challenge to love others well, we ought not to rely on our own understanding of how we ought to love—rather, we are to lean on Jesus to give us the ability to love the unlovable.*

PROCESS AND REFLECT: KINGDOM LOVE

1. What obstacles are you facing that may be hindering you from loving God more?
2. How do you intentionally receive the love of God each day?
3. There are no stipulations to earning the love of God. Why do you think we have a difficult time believing this?
4. Why is it so challenging to love our neighbors well?
5. What practical action step can you take to intentionally love someone who is challenging to love?

CHAPTER 4

Kingdom Unity

Jerusalem, built as a city should be, solidly united, where the tribes, the Lord's tribes, go up to give thanks to the name of the Lord.

—Ps 122:3–4

When I was in college, I went to one of the most incredible conferences of my life. It was called "The Passion Conference." This conference was held in Atlanta, and it hosted over sixty thousand college students under one dome. This might have been one of the most incredible physical expressions of what the kingdom of God would look like one day. There were thousands of people gathered who didn't know each other. They were all scattered around the country and globe, and they came together for a few days to experience the glory and majesty of God together. These college students gathered for one cause, and that cause was to worship the living Lord, Jesus Christ. The beauty in all of this was seeing the power of God manifested through the people of God as they came together in unison, lifting high the name of Jesus. To think that Jesus can bring about this kind of unity is remarkable. He offered salvation to those who would repent of their sins and believe in him as their Lord and Savior, so that they may have life abundant and life everlasting. Their sins would be forgiven as they would experience miraculous life change because of their Savior's work on the cross at Calvary. This is what unites the people of God. Our natural response to the work of Jesus must be worship. And worship is something that believers are called to do in everyday life but also together, in unity, not neglecting to meet together (Heb 10:24–25). Jesus gives his followers the ability to experience the glory of God that was given to him so that we would be united as one people (John 17:22–23). Our call is to be a kingdom people who are united for the cause of the gospel. If we are going to live our lives as kingdom people, who are united by the gospel of Jesus Christ, then we must learn to live in harmony with one another—even when our theological opinions differ.

COVENANT FAMILY

The church in America makes it easy for Christians to pick and choose a church of their liking. I have heard from many people that they go "church shopping." Now I am not here to knock on this. I think it is very important to find a church home where we will be able to grow in our walk with Jesus the most. Growing in our faith and growing in our relationship with Jesus is vital to our spiritual formation. But once we've committed to a church—ideally—that church becomes our church family. It is the place where we do life with other followers of Jesus. It is a place where the messiness of our lives and our past, present, and future circumstances are shared with other brothers and sisters in the Lord Jesus. We come together in worship, fellowship, prayer, and communion—and through all of these things, we grow into deeper intimacy with our risen Lord. Sharing life with people can be messy. When we open up with another follower of Jesus, we vulnerably invite them into some of our life's deepest wounds, pains, and sins. We also invite them to share in the joys, celebrations, and victories of our lives. The hope is this: that we would share life together; whether messy or beautiful, we would share it all. This beautiful picture of the church was so wonderfully demonstrated when the church was established in Acts. The author of Acts, Luke, writes this:

> They devoted themselves to the apostles' teaching, to the fellowship, to the breaking of bread, and to prayer. Everyone was filled with awe, and many wonders and signs were being performed through the apostles. Now all the believers were together and held all things in common. They sold their possessions and property and distributed the proceeds to all, as any had need. Every day they devoted themselves to meeting together in the temple, and broke bread from house to house. They ate their food with joyful

and sincere hearts, praising God and enjoying the favor of all the people. Every day the Lord added to their number those who were being saved. (Acts 2:42–47)

This is such a beautiful picture of the church, or as I like to call it, *the covenant family*. A covenant family is filled with followers of Jesus who unequivocally devote themselves to the apostles' teaching. Or as one commentator puts it, "The gathered community listened to and followed the preaching and teaching of the twelve apostles from—and based on—the Scriptures."[1] This covenant family broke bread together, shared meals, and were committed to prayer. They were filled with awe as they saw the incredible miracles that God was doing through his people. They held all things in common, such as possessions and property, so that they would help those in need in their covenant family. Their hearts were joyful and sincere, giving praise to the God who saved them and gave them life eternal. This kind of covenant family was an incredible witness to a broken world that was longing for hope. "Every day the Lord added to their number those who were being saved" (Acts 2:47). What a beautiful testimony it is to see the power of God working through the people of God for the glory of God and his kingdom. And when a broken world looks in, it sees that something different is going on in the church. There is a group of people who gather as a covenant family and share in life with each other. The God they worship and pray to is actively moving in their midst and giving them the strength needed to grow in their faith. The kind of community that is found in a covenant family demonstrates something so eccentric and profound. This is all possible because the hearts of the people who make up the covenant family are committed to kingdom unity. They are committed to not giving up on one another. They are in it for the long haul because community and fellowship matter. They are in it because family matters. Especially when family is rooted and grounded in the person and work of Jesus Christ. There are a variety of reasons why people in the church don't stick together through thick and thin. I've decided to highlight *some* of the problems.

PROBLEM: A SEVERED FAMILY

When my wife and I got married on May 24, 2014, we made a covenant before God and before a plethora of witnesses that we were committed to

---

1. Barry et al., *Faithlife Study Bible*, Acts 2:42.

each other. For better or for worse, for richer or for poorer, in sickness and in health. The intent on the wedding day is that we would hold to the promises that were made to one another—God as our ultimate witness. Since our marriage began, we have gone through many hills and valleys. There have been times when our marriage was tried by fire. Would we continue to hold on and make it through? Would we continue to say, "I am committed to you, through the good times and the bad times?" Marriage is hard. It requires work. It requires sacrifice. It requires me to say that I am wrong (even though I am always right). If you take yourself too seriously, you may not have understood that joke. Both spouses will make mistakes in the sanctity of marriage, but the hope is that regardless of the mistakes, both will be committed to working together—in unity—to continue to pursue beautiful and harmonious unity with one another. Christian marriage is an incredible witness to unbelievers of what Christ as the cornerstone can truly accomplish through fallen people. He binds us. He unites us. He gives us the ability to walk through the hardships together. He gives us the strength to persevere, even when we may feel like giving up. This is because Jesus is our cornerstone. He is the firm foundation that Christian marriage is intended to be built upon.

What we discussed previously regarding a covenant family is the ideal. It is the goal. It is what followers of Jesus ought to aspire toward. But we live in a world where sin is still living and active, and it penetrates the very covenant that we are called to unite in. The enemy loves to feast on the possibility of bringing division among the people of God. The secular world is already divisive enough. Everyone is fighting for a right or a cause, and if someone does not agree with that cause, they become enemies. People bash each other. Relationships are sacrificed. And then, we take a good look at the Christian church, and sometimes—not always, but sometimes—the church looks no different than the secular world. Toxic division exists among the people of God. The very people who are recipients of God's grace in salvation are the very people who are driving wedges in relationships in Christian churches. Whether it be politics, theology, ideology, hermeneutics, or personal preference—to name just a few—division is tearing up the church of Jesus Christ. This is not how it was intended to be. Scripture talks about this very topic. When Paul was on his second missionary journey, he received word about the quarreling among the Corinthian believers (1 Cor 1:11). People in the Corinthian church were claiming to be following the *correct* rules and the *correct* doctrines, and everyone was in disagreement. Paul writes:

> Now I urge you, brothers and sisters, in the name of our Lord Jesus Christ, that all of you agree in what you say, that there be no divisions among you, and that you be united with the same understanding and the same conviction. For it has been reported to me about you, my brothers and sisters, by members of Chloe's people, that there is rivalry among you. What I am saying is this: One of you says, "I belong to Paul," or "I belong to Apollos," or "I belong to Cephas," or "I belong to Christ." Is Christ divided? Was Paul crucified for you? Or were you baptized in Paul's name? (1 Cor 1:10–13)

What we see here is a form of tribalism. People are taking sides because they cannot agree with one another. This tribalism is splitting the church in Corinth and leading people into thinking that they are correct, while everyone else is incorrect. The common cause that Christ gave his life for is no longer the thing that is binding this community together. One commentator puts it this way, "Paul's rhetorical question challenges the Corinthians regarding the divisions within their congregation. Since Christ is one with His body, the Corinthian church (which Paul calls 'the body'; 12:27) should be united."[2] Instead, the Corinthians find themselves at odds with one another, causing division and disunity.

    If Christians are trying to reach their communities for Christ; if Christians are trying to reach their nation for Christ; if Christians are trying to reach the globe for Christ, how will this be possible, when the local church is having a difficult time getting along with itself? When the covenant family is confronted with challenges. When the covenant family disagrees on matters that are not central to historic Christian orthodoxy—how will unity be able to be preserved? The Christian church is made up of many people who come from many different backgrounds, experiences, denominations, theological differences, and so on. And the thing that unites everyone together is the person of Jesus Christ. Jesus Christ is the light in a dark world (John 8:12). He is the only one who can save people from their depravity (Acts 4:11–12). Jesus is the source of everlasting life (John 5:24). Yet this is not sufficient for all. We begin to say Jesus plus this or that equals a healthy church environment. And when certain standards are not met, the covenant family is severed. It begins to break. What was intended to be one

---

2. Barry et al., *Faithlife Study Bible*, 1 Cor 1:13.

beautiful and unified body of believers becomes a severed body that splits and separates for the cause of having self-proclaimed *right* and *proper* theology. There needs to be a better option to keep the church together in unison. There needs to be a better option so that the gospel can be faithfully expressed through the local church. Rather than dividing over secondary doctrines, the church must yearn to unite over that which initially brought the church together.

> Rather than dividing over secondary doctrines, the church must yearn to unite over that which initially brought the church together.

A PROBLEM: AN ATTEMPT TO UNDERSTAND THE BIBLE

There is no doubt that a plethora of theological positions and understandings exist within the Christian church. People read the Bible and come to different conclusions about what certain texts mean. Some read it with presuppositions—that is, they bring preconceived notions to the text and assume that the text means something that it may not mean. Some read every word with a literal nature—which means when they read the Bible, they take what every passage says literally. Others will take verses out of context to help support a particular stance, narrative, or agenda that they may be trying to push. E. Randolph Richards and Brandon J. O'Brien wrote a very helpful book entitled *Misreading Scripture with Western Eyes: Removing Cultural Blinders to Better Understand the Bible*. In it, they write:

> Christians always and everywhere have believed that the Bible is the Word of God. God spoke in the past, "through the prophets at many times and in various ways," and most clearly by his Son (Heb 1:1). By the Holy Spirit, God continues to speak to his people through the Scriptures. It is important that Christ's church retain this conviction, even as it poses certain challenges for interpretation. We can easily forget that Scripture is a foreign land and that reading the Bible is a cross-cultural experience. To open the Word of God is to step into a strange world where things are very unlike our own. Most of us don't speak the languages. We don't know the geography or the customs or what behaviors are considered rude or polite. And yet we hardly notice. For many of us, the Bible is more familiar than any other book. We may have parts of it memorized. And because we believe that the Bible is God's Word

to us, no matter where on the planet or when in history we read it, we tend to read Scripture in our own *when* and *where*, in a way that makes sense on our terms. We believe the Bible has something to say to us today. We read the words, "you are . . . neither hot nor cold" to mean what they mean to us: that you are neither spiritually hot or spiritually cold. As we will see, it is a better method to speak of what the passage meant to the original hearers, and then to ask how that applies to us. Another way to say this is that all Bible reading is necessarily contextual.[3]

That may be a lot to ingest, but we must understand this when it comes to interpreting the Bible. When reading the Bible, we must read it contextually to derive the most faithful meaning that may apply to us. When reading the Bible we must ask, "Who is the author? Who is the audience receiving the letter from the author? Why is the author writing this letter to this specific audience? What is happening culturally and contextually? Where is the location of the audience?" When we can answer these questions while reading the Biblical text, then the meaning of the text becomes more vibrant and effective. It is translated more faithfully. We can then begin to comprehend the substance of what a certain passage means. And when we can do that, we can find applications for our lives today. When we don't understand these things, our translation of the text can be murky at best. Let me illustrate.

I have the incredible privilege of serving a church family in central Wisconsin. When my wife and I moved to central Wisconsin, we came because God had me in a discipleship pastor role. I had hoped to serve in this role for a significant amount of years. Well, after my serving as the discipleship pastor for just over a year, the former lead pastor informed our church that he would be stepping away, as the Lord was calling his family to another ministry assignment. For some odd reason, God, in his humorous ways, thought it would be a good idea for me to candidate for the lead pastor role. And it is by God's grace alone that the church extended the call for me to serve them in this role. Now if the former pastor had written me a letter, put it in the mail, and the letter arrived at another pastor's home, here is how I would presume it would go. The greeting of the letter would address me, not the current recipient of the letter. The letter might share ministry experiences that I shared with the former pastor. The letter might have words of encouragement. The letter may contain memories that

---

3. Richards and O'Brien, *Misreading Scripture*, 11.

we shared in ministry. Perhaps some encouragement in my ministry and a farewell. Since the letter was not received by me, the intended audience, the other recipient could perhaps interpret and translate some of the statements from the letter for him or herself. There may be similar ministry experiences that would be relatable in a different context. But if the pastor who obtained the letter knew who the writer of the letter was and the original recipient of that letter, a greater meaning and understanding would be formed. If the context of the letter was understood, the letter would make more sense. This is why it is so vital to do our homework as those who are trying to understand the Bible. We need to put everything in context to best understand what it all means for us today. When we do this, we will get a much better understanding of what the passages of the Bible mean.

This, of course, is the goal. The goal is to be sure that we can understand God's word most accurately and faithfully. Even still, we have many who come from a variety of denominational backgrounds, life experiences, and theological presuppositions, which inform their understanding of the Bible and can often bring conflict to the church. I would argue that even in the midst of this, we can still worship together as a kingdom-minded people, if and only if we are willing to *humble* ourselves before God and allow for God to work in our hearts. What if instead of looking for ways to prove ourselves right, we simply submit ourselves to what unites and binds us together in perfect harmony as the Christian church? Again, disagreements and disunity are nothing new under the sun. This posture predates our modern-day issues. We already looked at the disunity in Corinth. I am a firm believer that kingdom unity is possible within a kingdom people. To me, kingdom unity is a symbol of what life in the kingdom looks like. The kingdom is a place where professed followers of Jesus will spend eternity together. Our call is to seek first the kingdom of God (Matt 6:33). But we can get so caught up in the weeds of theology and doctrine that we neglect and reject one another along the way. I am not saying that theology and doctrine are not important. They are extremely important. People should have stances and take positions based on biblical convictions. But to experience kingdom unity here on earth, followers of Jesus must learn how

> What if instead of looking for ways to prove ourselves right, we simply submit ourselves to what unites and binds us together in perfect harmony as the Christian church?

to live in covenant with one another. When disagreements arise, we must work together in not allowing them to sever our fellowship. This is what the enemy desires and is after. And when we give in, the enemy will divide the Christian church from within. The enemy will dismember the many body parts that make up the one body called the church. We must be committed to one another. We must be committed to the gospel. We must be committed to what holds the church together. We must not give the enemy room to divide us, as we long to minister the gospel of grace to a broken and hurting world. Even though different perspectives exist when it comes to understanding theology and the Bible, we must be committed to the main thing as our source of kingdom unity.

A SOLUTION? THE APOSTLES' CREED

Throughout the history of the church, many followers of Jesus agreed and disagreed on a variety of matters concerning the things of God. To maintain faithful Christian orthodoxy, the Apostles' Creed was produced. This creed was meant to represent the "core teachings" of the Christian faith. In it, everything that a regenerated follower of Jesus needs to know is found. For those unfamiliar with the Apostles' Creed, here is what it declares:

> I believe in God the Father almighty, creator of heaven and earth; And in Jesus Christ, His only Son, our Lord, Who was conceived by the Holy Spirit, born from the Virgin Mary, suffered under Pontius Pilate, was crucified, dead and buried, descended into hell, on the third day rose again from the dead, ascended to heaven, sits at the right hand of God the Father almighty, thence He will come to judge the living and the dead; I believe in the Holy Spirit, the holy Catholic Church, the communion of saints, the remission of sins, the resurrection of the flesh, and eternal life. Amen.[4]

This statement holds the core beliefs and teachings of Christian orthodoxy. This means that everything in it gives followers of Jesus insight into what cannot be disputed or argued over as the main framework of Christian theology. The Apostles' Creed grounds the Christian faith and provides followers of Jesus with the understanding of what primary doctrine must consist of. A Logos article on the Apostles' Creed states:

---

4. See Logos Staff, "Apostles' Creed."

> The Apostles' Creed seems to represent some form of what the early church called the "rule of faith." The early Christians were guided by the "rule of faith," the Holy Spirit working in community and individuals, and the authoritative Scriptures. Before the "rule of faith" was called such, there were general references to the teachings and traditions of the apostles. It is these core teachings that seem to make up the Apostles' Creed....
>
> The Apostles' Creed represents a set of uncompromisable core beliefs for Christians. As such, the core tradition of it is also found in the Nicene Creed. The Apostles' Creed, like all creeds, functions like a filter for orthodoxy; it indicates what is and what is not "Christian." It is a public profession of belief in historic Christianity.[5]

The Apostles' Creed is a very helpful affirmation and resource into what the Christian church must hold to in its doctrine and theology. If we get the things of the creed wrong, our Christian orthodoxy is violated. Kingdom unity must be rooted in these theological principles as the basic ground rules for the Christian faith. The Apostles' Creed grounds followers of Jesus in a Trinitarian theology that understands God as Father, Son, and Holy Spirit. It grounds followers of Jesus to understand the incarnation of Jesus Christ, who was born of a virgin and needed to become one of us so that he could reconcile humanity to a holy God and set us free from the bondage and grip of sin in our lives. Without the incarnation, Jesus would not have been crucified on a Roman cross, buried, and physically raised from the dead. The creed also explains the holistic nature of the gospel. It gives insight into the person and work of Jesus Christ. The things mentioned in the creed are essential for Christian theology. These are the things the church *must* unite on. It is what holds faithful orthodoxy together.

So if the church's foundation is Jesus and the core Christian doctrines include the Trinity, the incarnation of Jesus, and the holistic understanding of the gospel (Jesus's birth, life, death, burial, resurrection, ascension, and return), then why does the church find itself living in disunity? Why is kingdom unity so difficult to pursue, and why can't we agree on our core roots? I believe that disunity in the Christian church exists when followers of Jesus decide to major in the minors. When secondary doctrine begins to creep into primary doctrine. When the foundations that are found in the Apostles' Creed are not enough for Christian orthodoxy. This is often at the core of theological disunity in the church. It makes the church look

---

5. Logos Staff, "Apostles' Creed."

less like a kingdom church and more like a church in a broken world. We must strive as followers of Jesus to uphold the bride of Christ as sacred and beautiful. We must strive as followers of Jesus to pursue unity with one another, rather than walking away when we disagree with something. We must long to see a church on earth as it is in heaven. When a broken and hurting world is desperate for hope, let us not create environments that feed it with hopelessness. Let us be a people who portray kingdom unity.

KINGDOM UNITY

I like a good song. I like to jam out in the car sometimes—especially when no one is looking—to some of my favorite songs. When someone sees me, I pretend like everything is perfectly normal and I'm just driving to my location. I remember rocking out to a song once, and then I pulled up to a red light, totally lost in the beauty of my voice. I looked over, and the car next to me had an individual behind the wheel who was simply cracking up at the fact that I was singing at the top of my lungs. Here's the best part: I can't sing well to save my life. I pretend like I can when it's just me, myself, and I.

Songs were a powerful expression in biblical times. Many biblical writers would sing as they worshiped God. Lots of them would write their songs down. Thankfully, we have been graced with the opportunity to read some of these songs in the Scriptures. There is an entire section in Psalms that is known as the *psalms of ascent*. These were songs that the people of Israel would sing to God on their journey toward Jerusalem for annual feasts and festivals. During one of the songs of worship (Ps 122), the psalmist lets out incredible expressions of worship toward the Lord. But there is a specific statement that was very profound when it came to worship. The psalmist writes, "Jerusalem, built as a city should be, solidly united, where the tribes, the Lord's tribes, go up to give thanks to the name of the Lord" (Ps 122:3–4). Eugene Peterson gives a great understanding of what was happening in these verses:

> In Jerusalem everything that God said was remembered and celebrated. When you went to Jerusalem, you encountered the great foundational realities: God created you, God redeemed you, God provided for you. In Jerusalem you saw in ritual and heard proclaimed in preaching the powerful history-shaping truth that God forgives our sins and makes it possible to live without guilt and with purpose. In Jerusalem all the scattered fragments of

> experience, all the bits and pieces of truth and feeling and perception were put together in a single whole.[6]

What I love about Peterson's commentary here is that he reminds us that in Jerusalem, you encountered the great foundational realities: God created you, God redeemed you, and God provided for you. This is what grounded the people of God together. Regardless of their experiences and backgrounds, they were all united as one kingdom people for the glory and worship of God. They were committed to demonstrating what it looked like to be one body for one cause. They put their differences aside for the sake of something bigger. They were going before the presence of a holy God. They were going to encounter God's powerful presence being manifested in their lives. They were going to be nourished by their Creator—being reminded of God's faithfulness toward his people. Their theological disagreements did not get in the way of who they were uniting to worship together. Jerusalem was built as a city should be, solidly united, where tribes, the Lord's tribes go up to give thanks to the name of the Lord (Ps 122:3–4). The architectural strength of the city was also true of the people who came to worship there. Peterson continues:

> In worship all the different tribes functioned as a single people in harmonious relationship. In worship, though we have come from different places and out of various conditions, we are demonstrably after the same things, saying the same things, doing the same things. With all our differing levels of intelligence and wealth, background and language, rivalries and resentments, still in worship we are gathered into a single whole. Outer quarrels and misunderstandings and differences pale into insignificance as the inner unity of what God builds in the act of worship is demonstrated.[7]

This is a perfect image of what kingdom unity looks like. One day, when our time on earth is done and the Lord calls us home, our differences will not define us. We will be defined by the person of Jesus Christ—just as we are here on earth. He alone is who we aspire to know. He alone is who we aspire to be like. He is our source of life. And it is Jesus alone who we worship as his followers. But we tend to replace the worship of Jesus with the worship of our theological, political, or personal ideologies.

---

6. Peterson, *Long Obedience*, 45–46.
7. Peterson, *Long Obedience*, 46.

One of the most incredible experiences that I've had as a Christian pastor is something that happens with all of the evangelical churches in the city of Marshfield, Wisconsin. On Good Friday, the evangelical churches come together, meet, and plan a Good Friday service that is put on by all of the churches. The churches involved include a variety of denominations. Each denomination is nuanced by certain theological differences, but that does not hold anyone back from the ultimate goal and mission—to worship Jesus Christ crucified. The way that all of the staff from every church works together to help foster a service that helps people come together in kingdom unity is simply beautiful. It is truly unlike anything that I had experienced in ministry before moving to Marshfield. During my first experience of this, I remember looking around the room and seeing pastors from each church united as one people. The room filled with followers of Jesus lifting high his glorious name, reminiscing on the weight of the cross for our sins together. We sing, we pray, we listen, we repent, and we experience—all of this—in kingdom unity. I left the experience thinking, wow, that was a glimpse of what a united kingdom of Jesus followers is going to look like one day.

A PLEA FOR HOPE

So if this is a picture of kingdom unity, why do followers of Jesus not strive for this in our churches? Why do we allow our disagreements to drive a wedge between us and other faithful followers of Jesus? Why can we not work together as a covenant family, seeking resolve? When needed, we can agree to disagree so long as we are rooted in the essentials of the Christian faith as demonstrated in the Apostles' Creed. How much more would a broken and hurting world be compelled by the reconciling gospel of Jesus Christ? What they see in the church is something unique, special, and beautiful. Where the lost see a place where they can be found. Where people who are living in a hopeless world can find hope in the gospel and in the people of God—who are ushering in that hope. I believe that lives would be transformed and people would experience a life-changing God in their own lives. I believe the church would have a better reputation than it has in this modern age. How beautiful would it be if everyone who claimed Jesus Christ as their Lord and Savior would dwell together in unity and harmony for the cause of the gospel? Or as the psalmist writes in a psalm of ascent, "How good and pleasant it is when God's people live together in unity" (Ps

133:1 NIV). Let us be kingdom people. A kingdom people who are striving to pursue unity within the church. The gospel is the source that binds us together as followers of Jesus. When we have petty disagreements that lead to the severing of the members of the church, we give a poor demonstration of what a kingdom people look like to the world around us. Let's work on being a different kind of church. If we profess Jesus Christ as our Lord and Savior, let us be committed to the cause of Christ and the cause of Christ's bride, the church. If the church is going to be the light of the world, then let us be a church that looks differently than the world. Let us not divide among ourselves. Let us find harmonious beauty in worshiping our Lord and Savior together, as we faithfully witness the good news of Jesus to all.

> *If the church is going to be the light of the world, then let us be a church that looks differently than the world.*

PROCESS AND REFLECT: KINGDOM UNITY

1. Why do you think it is so challenging for the Christian church to get along?

2. How have you seen church division play a role in influencing your spiritual walk?

3. What personal measures can you take to help bring your local church into kingdom unity?

4. We all bring baggage into the church. How can we intentionally avoid our preconceived biases and strive to live in harmony with other believers?

PART THREE: A Kingdom Experience

CHAPTER 5

Kingdom Presence

God, you are my God; I eagerly seek you. I thirst for you; my body faints for you in a land that is dry, desolate, and without water. So I gaze on you in the sanctuary to see your strength and your glory. My lips will glorify you because your faithful love is better than life.

—Ps 63:1–3

I AM NOT THE thrill-seeking type. There are many things in life that I enjoy, but thrill-seeking never seems appealing to me. Part of this could very well be that I usually default to fear when I think of doing seemingly dangerous activities. I spent my entire childhood avoiding roller coasters because I was not interested in the thrill of them. All of my friends would spend their days at Six Flags, while I would bow out so that I could stay at home and not fear for my life. I was once told that if I don't try something, how can I truly know what it is like? Well, in 2011, I was interning at a church in the western suburbs of Chicago. While I was there, the youth ministry would do something called Fun Fridays. On Fun Fridays, students in the high school ministry would go and participate in an activity. As a leadership team, we had planned a variety of activities that the youth would set out to participate in. One of which included going to Six Flags Great America. I remember thinking in my head of any excuses that I could come up with so that I did not have to attend this horrendous event. But there was nothing that would work. I had to go. So I went.

While at Six Flags I still attempted to find a way out of going on a roller coaster, so I convinced my youth pastor that I would stay back with some of the students and their belongings. This worked . . . for a little while. Suddenly a student who was trying to overcome his fear approached me and said, "Rob, will you go on a roller coaster with me?" I remember at that moment thinking, this is it, my life is over if I say yes. I'm too young to die. I don't want to do this. I don't know what came over me, but I decided to go with this student. The anticipation of waiting in line had my entire body feeling something it never had felt in the past. There was absolute fear encapsulating every part of me. After waiting in line for nearly an hour, it was our time. We were up. I sat on the roller coaster, my palms began to sweat, and the roller coaster began moving. As soon as it began to go up, I looked at the student and said, "I don't feel very good." He looked at me and reminded me that we had barely moved. The roller coaster began to accelerate in speed while it started to climb higher and higher. There it was, death was at the doorway. We hit the highest peak. It was like being on top of a mountain and looking over the beautiful horizon. Except the roller coaster wasn't planning on staying put. Next thing you know, I am looking down and the roller coaster begins to make a downward shift. All of a sudden the roller coaster completely drops down, at full speed, with no looking back, all while my stomach is in my mouth. I was uncontrollably screaming at the top of my lungs, and I was not sure what was happening. I was experiencing the thrill of a lifetime. Shortly after, the ride was over. When everything had calmed and settled, the roller coaster parked itself back where it had started. I stepped out and couldn't feel my legs. What just happened? I did it! I survived! The experience was exhilarating and something that I will always remember. This would not be the case if I had not given roller coasters a chance. I had decided to experience something I had never experienced in my life.

> *When we want to experience the presence of God, we must take the initiative in pursuing his presence.*

When we want to experience the presence of God, we must take the initiative in pursuing his presence. God dwells in our midst, but if we don't take a step toward him, we may not be able to experience the power of his presence. To fully experience the power of the presence of God, we must actively seek him, and when we do, he will reveal himself to us. The first step in encountering the presence of God is faith.

KINGDOM FAITH

Throughout this book, we have been aspiring to be kingdom people. A people who are being transformed on earth as it is in heaven. To be kingdom people, we must believe in the kingdom's cause. Believing in the kingdom's cause requires faith and trust in God, knowing that he is doing extraordinary work in our midst. How do we take that step of faith knowing that God is on the throne and that he is working in our midst? I believe this is found in Solomon's wisdom to his son: "Trust in the Lord with all your heart, and do not rely on your own understanding; in all your ways know him, and he will make your paths straight" (Prov 3:5–6). Here we see Solomon starting with the word "trust." This word "trust" here is the Hebrew word *bāṭaḥ* (בָּטַח) and can be translated as "to trust, trust in, to have confidence, be confident, to be bold, to be secure."[1] So to put our trust in the Lord means to put our absolute confidence in him. We do this not with some of our heart but as Solomon writes, "with all your heart" (Prov 3:5). Everything that is in us. We must completely put our dependence on God, trusting that he is on the throne and that he is in control. We do this by not relying on our own understanding (Prov 3:5). When we attempt to rely on our own understanding, we can tend to trust in ourselves as the primary captains of our ship. This should not be the case when it comes to trusting God. When we put our trust in God, we deny ourselves and completely and confidently defer our lives into his hands. This is why we must strive—in all of our ways—to know him. When we know him, we get to experience him. When we experience God, we can't help but surrender ourselves in worship to him. Worship is the natural overflow of our trust in the God of the universe.

CREATED FOR WORSHIP

Every single one of us was created for worship. This is who we were made to be. But so often, we find ourselves bowing down to the many idols in this life. Instead of choosing to worship God, we choose to worship materialism, money, promotions, people, security, our image, our approval from others, government, success, personal accolades, and this list can go on and on. With the right heart and intent, none of these things are bad. But when we make them our source of worship—something we adore and give reverence to—and spend more time fixated on these things than on God, then

---

1. See https://www.blueletterbible.org/lexicon/h982/csb/wlc/0-1/.

they become our idols. As people who were created to worship, we have a daily decision to make regarding who or what we will choose to worship. Will we choose to worship the things that this world has to offer? Or will it be Jesus Christ, who came to conquer sin and death, giving us everlasting life in him? We must be people who worship the Creator, not the creation. When we do this, our lives will be transformed. When we worship the Creator, we give the Creator room to mold us, shape us, and conform us to the image of God that we were created to be. When we worship our Creator, we give God room to operate on us—so that our hearts would be completely renovated.

> *When we worship the Creator, we give the Creator room to mold us, shape us, and conform us to the image of God that we were created to be.*

A RENOVATED HEART

A couple of years back, my wife and I were able to purchase our first-ever home. It was an old farmhouse that was over 125 years old. When we walked through the home, we immediately fell in love. This was the one. This was the place that we would call home. Once we moved in, we found out that we were having our second child. When we considered the layout of our home, we recognized that though we loved this home, we had a complex bedroom situation. We had one bedroom for a child, but adding to our family would complicate things, as there wasn't a definitive space for another child. Our church is incredible. They knew that our family was growing, and one gentleman in particular thought it would be a good idea to add onto our house, adding two extra bedrooms for our growing family. A group of very remarkable people stepped up and began to renovate our home so that we would be able to add two more rooms. When the renovations began, this house that we fell in love with was looking rough. The roof was ripped off. The walls were torn down. Dust was everywhere. The floors were removed. Windows were taken out. It was looking less and less like the home that we had first bought. I remember when my wife and I were talking, we were thankful that the project was underway, but it was a struggle to be home during the renovations. Fast forward three months. Our home was complete. The two rooms were officially added, painted, and put together. All of the debris was gone. The house was clean and furnished, awaiting the birth of our baby girl. All of the hard work was on display to be seen. The house we had bought was no longer the house we were living in. It was new. It was fresh. It was better than we could have ever imagined.

If we think about our lives as followers of Jesus, our hearts are constantly in the renovation process. They are constantly being worked on and made new by the Holy Spirit. Who we once were is not who we are today, because the Spirit of the living God dwells within us. The Spirit of the living God transforms us by the grace of God, giving us a new inward nature. Although things can be messy, feeling like debris is all over the place, the end goal of the renovation of our hearts is that we would be more like Christ. Becoming more like Christ means that we are becoming the kingdom people we were created to be. It is in the renovation process that we learn that we aren't who we were intended to be, but we are being transformed into who we are supposed to be. This does not take away from who we are right now. We are precious in the sight of God. We are all unique and different from one another—and this shows the creativity of our Creator. Sin works hard at distorting us so that we would fall into the trap of worshiping the things of this world. The renovation of our hearts by the Holy Spirit is essential for our spiritual formation to thrive here on earth as it will be in heaven. When we are formed by the power of the Holy Spirit, we become more like Christ and less like our sinful selves. Truly recognizing the need for our renovation will create in us a desperation for Jesus as the source of life. When Jesus becomes the source of our lives, we can't help but fall down and worship him. In our genuine expression of worship toward Jesus, we can encounter his powerful presence.

THE PRESENCE OF GOD

There is nothing more powerful than the presence of God. When the presence of God is encountered, lives are transformed. Throughout the Old Testament, God's presence was localized. God spoke to Moses and instructed that a tabernacle be built so that his presence would dwell there (Exod 25:1–9). God gave instructions on everything that would be included in the tabernacle, including the ark of the covenant (Exod 25:10–22), the table for the bread of the presence (Exod 25:23–30), and the lampstand (Exod 25:31–40). This would be the makeup of what was entailed for a successful tabernacle. The tabernacle (מִשְׁכָּן) was a tent that was constructed during

Kingdom Formation

the Israelites' wanderings in the wilderness.[2] As the presence of God would dwell in the tabernacle, high priests, or God's appointed people, would be the primary individuals who would be able to access the presence of God. When they did, they would communicate God's word to the people of Israel. The tabernacle was a place where God would be encountered in many ways. The *New Dictionary of Biblical Theology* states:

> The first sanctuary mentioned in the OT was a portable construction. 2 Samuel 7:6 appears to summarize the accounts of the tent sanctuary. In his word to David God said, I have not dwelt in a house since the day I brought up the people of Israel from Egypt to this day, but I have been moving about in a tent for my dwelling. The story of the Tabernacle begins at Mt Sinai, at the ratification of the covenant (Ex 24). Directions for its construction follow in Exodus 25–31. It is an elaborate construction and serves several purposes. It is the place where God dwells in the midst of his people (Ex 25:8). It also serves as the place of divine revelation (Ex 25:22), and it is here that sacrifices are offered and atonement is made (Ex 29:38–43; 30:7–10).[3]

Here we see the variety of functions that the tabernacle served. Although God worked in powerful ways through the tabernacle, God's presence was not accessible to all. It was, however, taken all over the place. The tabernacle was designed in a way that it could be torn down, moved, and set up elsewhere—and God's presence would dwell again. Later in Israel's history, King Solomon built the first stationary temple—where the presence of God would dwell in Jerusalem (1 Kgs 6). This stationary temple would be the new dwelling place of God among the people of Israel. This temple certainly served its purpose but did not last long. The temple Solomon had built would be destroyed as the Babylonians took Israel into captivity (2 Kgs 25:9). After these events, there was another attempt at rebuilding the temple. This would be known as the Second Temple, and yet again, it would house the presence of God.

Jesus would come and change the entire landscape when it came to the presence of God. Jesus came to usher in the presence of God beyond the temple and tabernacle. In the Old Testament, the temple was the key place of worship, and that's where God would dwell. The work of Jesus overturns the old covenant and the need for infrastructure to house the presence of God.

---

2. Hyun, "Tabernacle."

3. Rosner et al., *New Dictionary*, 806.

Kingdom Presence

Immediately following the death of Jesus, something profound happened. The Gospel writer Matthew records it this way, "Jesus cried out again with a loud voice and gave up his spirit. Suddenly, the curtain of the sanctuary was torn in two from top to bottom, the earth quaked, and the rocks were split" (Matt 27:50–51). Behind the curtain was where the presence of God would manifest itself in the temple. The moment that Jesus breathed his last, the curtain that gave access to the presence of God in the sanctuary, tore. Something new was transpiring. When the tearing of the curtain occurred, it demonstrated profound symbolism that the earthly temple was quickly approaching its expiration date. This means that Jesus himself is the new temple—the new most holy place—with no curtain separating us from intimacy with him. As followers of Jesus, we have complete access to encounter the living God. God's presence is no longer confined to a particular place. In fact, by way of the Holy Spirit, followers of Jesus can access the presence of God at all times and in all places. When Paul was addressing the church in Corinth, he specifically made a statement regarding the human body as the dwelling place of the Holy Spirit. Paul writes, "Don't you know that your body is a temple of the Holy Spirit who is in you, whom you have from God? You are not your own, for you were bought at a price. So glorify God with your body" (1 Cor 6:19–20). Jesus bought us with a price, having his body broken and blood shed so that we may have eternal life. Part of our participation in eternal life on earth is being the residence where the Holy Spirit dwells. As the Spirit dwells within us, we experience the presence of God among us. In Christ, we can confidently say that God will never leave us nor forsake us (Heb 13:5). This is especially powerful because only a few people in biblical times had surreal encounters with God. These were called *theophanies*. The *New Dictionary of Biblical Theology* states:

> Many times in biblical history God appeared in human form or revealed himself through the elements of nature. Sometimes he appeared to people when they were fully awake; at other times he revealed himself in a dream to someone asleep or in a trance. Such tangible instances of divine self-revelation are called theophanies. Biblical poets often depict God coming in the storm in his role of warrior-king. These poetic descriptions are often purely literary, reflecting the poet's theological interpretation of an experience or event, not an actual divine appearance. But in other cases a poetic description is based on a literal divine appearance.[4]

---

4. Rosner et al., *New Dictionary*, 815–16.

So as we see here, God's presence would be experienced in a variety of ways throughout the Old Testament. People would encounter God in unique ways. God can still speak to us and appear to us in extraordinary ways, but we can be assured that our bodies are the dwelling place for the Holy Spirit. God ventures through life with us. We are never left to walk alone. By putting our faith and trust in Jesus, we receive the gift of the Holy Spirit—who nourishes our souls, guides our steps, convicts our sins, and manifests the presence of God. Since we have the presence of the living God dwelling within us, we can pursue deeper encounters with him. The more we encounter the presence of God on earth, the more we will know God intimately in preparation for kingdom life that goes beyond this earth. Next, we will look at some practical ways we can experience the presence of God through daily spiritual habits.

SPIRITUAL HABITS

I have a few close friends. Emphasis on *few*. The older I get, the fewer friends I have. I am using this opportunity to ask if you will be my friend. Please reach out and let me know if you accept this challenge of friendship with me. I used to live near one of my very close friends. After my family moved from Chicago in 2020, my friend and his family moved to Michigan. Geographically, we grew further apart. It has forced us to be intentional in our communication so that our friendship would continue to grow. Once a year, we make it a point to have both of our families meet in a similar geographical location so that we can spend quality time together. What I learned in our distance is that when you want to know someone, you need to make an effort to pursue friendship and relationship with them. This is something that my friend and I decided that we would be committed to. This commitment on both ends is important so that our relationship will be preserved. Not only that, but we would be able to grow deeper in our friendship through being intentional with one another.

One of the ways that followers of Jesus can grow in their relationship with Jesus is by being intentional with him. This requires work on our end to be sure to meet with and find Jesus. Though Jesus dwells within us by way of the Holy Spirit, we can easily forget that this is the case. And when we forget, we can quickly jump to the conclusion that God seems distant or that God seems far away from us. James writes, "Draw near to God, and he will draw near to you" (Jas 4:8). God is already near. When God feels far away from us, perhaps we need to look internally and ask, "Have I been intentional in connecting with God, or have I been drifting?" How we answer that question will reveal how distant we are from God. The moment we intentionally begin to pursue God is the moment we begin connecting, or reconnecting, with him. If we want to experience the presence of God in our lives, we must participate in daily spiritual rhythms that propel our connection with God. This is what we will be unpacking in the coming pages. Before we dig deeper, here are some practical ways that we can connect with the Creator of the universe: Scripture, solitude, prayer, fasting, taking the Sabbath and keeping it holy, reflection and meditation, serving, developing a worship lifestyle, and intentional community.

Scripture

One of the ways to connect with God and encounter his presence is through Scripture. The Gospel writer John writes, "In the beginning was the Word, and the Word was with God, and the Word was God" (John 1:1). We refer to the Scripture as the word of God because it is through the Scriptures that we can read, learn, encounter, and experience who God was, is, and always will be. Scripture informs us of the words that God gave to people throughout human history. It is God's very word that brought the world into existence. The creation account gives us a picture of this: "In the beginning, God created the heavens and the earth. Now the earth was formless and empty, darkness covered the surface of the watery depths, and the Spirit of God was hovering over the surface of the waters. Then God said, 'Let there be light,' and there was light" (Gen 1:1–3). When God spoke his word, the light was created. When God utters words from his mouth, supernatural realities come to fruition. God reveals himself to us by speaking words into life. When we consider the Scriptures, let us consider them as holy and sacred texts by which God communicates to us.

Scripture also reveals the person of Jesus to us, giving us the ability to know, receive, and give our lives over to Jesus. In Scripture, we have eyewitness testimonies of those who experienced Jesus and wrote down the marvelous works he did. When we invite the presence of the Holy Spirit into our Scripture reading, we are asking the God who created all things to personally meet with and engage with us. What an astounding reality! The God who made all things and breathed all things into existence gave us the ability to encounter him through the Holy Scriptures. The Scriptures may be one of the greatest gifts from God to humanity. In the Holy Scriptures, we get to encounter the character of God. We get to learn from God and how he worked—from the very beginning until now. God reveals his faithfulness to humanity through the pages of Scripture.

Scripture gives us the ability to stand firm and stand our ground while facing opposition from the enemy. The Gospel writer Matthew gives us a glimpse into Jesus's encounter with the enemy and how Jesus was rooted in what the Scriptures taught:

> Then Jesus was led up by the Spirit into the wilderness to be tempted by the devil. After he had fasted forty days and forty nights, he was hungry. Then the tempter approached him and said, "If you are the Son of God, tell these stones to become bread." He answered, "It is written: Man must not live on bread alone but on every word that comes from the mouth of God." Then the devil took him to the holy city, had him stand on the pinnacle of the temple, and said to him, "If you are the Son of God, throw yourself down. For it is written: He will give his angels orders concerning you, and they will support you with their hands so that you will not strike your foot against a stone." Jesus told him, "It is also written: Do not test the Lord your God." Again, the devil took him to a very high mountain and showed him all the kingdoms of the world and their splendor. And he said to him, "I will give you all these things if you will fall down and worship me." Then Jesus told him, "Go away, Satan! For it is written: Worship the Lord your God, and serve only him." Then the devil left him, and angels came and began to serve him. (Matt 4:1–11)

This is a wonderful account of the power that Jesus has in both the Scriptures and the resistance of the evil one. The enemy sees that Jesus is hungry. The enemy thinks that, because of this, Jesus is weak. The enemy attempts to dive headfirst into the fact that Jesus is fully human and is hungry due to fasting. The temptation that the enemy holds over Jesus's head is urging Jesus to use his power to turn stones into loaves of bread so that Jesus would no longer be hungry. Jesus responds with "It is written: Man must not live on bread alone but on every word that comes from the mouth of God" (Matt 4:4). Jesus held onto the truth of Scripture when he was confronted with opposition. He knew what he needed to do. Jesus was so in tune with the Scriptures that any attempt from the enemy to lead him off course was crushed. Three times, Jesus used Scripture accurately to resist the temptation of the evil one. Jesus persisted. He persisted until the work was complete. After being grounded in the Scripture, finally Jesus declares, "Go away, Satan! For it is written: Worship the Lord your God, and serve only him" (Matt 4:10). The result? The enemy leaves.

Scripture gives us the ability to do so many things, one of which is resisting the enemy. When we are attempting to faithfully follow the person of Jesus, there will be a massive target on our backs where the enemy will try to throw us off the course of following Jesus. We cannot give the enemy any room to operate. We must resist. When the enemy tries to enter into our lives, our families, our churches, our workplaces, or any other context that we are in, we must hold on to the powerful words of James, "Therefore, submit to God. Resist the devil, and he will flee from you" (Jas 4:7). One of the best ways to resist the devil is by being grounded in the Scripture.

The Scriptures feed our souls. They allow us to encounter the presence of God by reading about the many things that God has done in human history. God is never changing. The author of Hebrews writes that "Jesus Christ is the same yesterday, today, and forever." By understanding the Scriptures, we understand the very nature of who God is and how he desires to relate to us—his precious creation. When we encounter the Holy Scriptures, we encounter the very message that God desires to communicate to us. Let us be people who starve for the Scripture. Let us feast on the incredible gift that we have from our personal and intimate God. Let us be people of Scripture who seek to be satisfied by the power of God's word.

> By understanding the Scriptures, we understand the very nature of who God is and how he desires to relate to us—his precious creation.

Solitude

This spiritual rhythm can be one of the most challenging ones to be intentional about. In a world where we are constantly on the go, slowing down and participating in a time of solitude seems impossible. When we look at Jesus, we see he would often take time to step away and spend time in solitude. The Gospel writer Mark records this in his Gospel, "Very early in the morning, while it was still dark, he got up, went out, and made his way to a deserted place; and there he was praying" (Mark 1:35). Jesus found value in being in a deserted place while connecting with God through prayer.

Solitude can seem like a lonely place, but it is the exact opposite of that. Solitude is an experience with the God of the universe who gently, quietly, and peacefully meets with us, enabling us to be still and know that he is God. Solitude gives us the ability to quiet ourselves before God and give him room to speak to our hearts. Richard Foster writes in his book *Celebration of Discipline*, "The purpose of silence and solitude is to be able to see and hear. The Spirit speaks to us when our heart is still and silent before the Lord—not when we're rushing about and doing our own thing in our own way."[5] This, of course, is challenging when we live in a world that is constantly on the go. This is why practicing this spiritual habit is so vital. As followers of Jesus, we need to hear from God. How can we hear from God when there is so much noise all around us? God can do wonders if we invite him into our inner life. Tim Keller writes:

> Solitude is an experience with the God of the universe who gently, quietly, and peacefully meets with us, enabling us to be still and know that he is God.

> If we give priority to the outer life, our inner life will be dark and scary. We will not know what to do with solitude. We will be deeply uncomfortable with self-examination, and we will have an increasingly short attention span for any kind of reflection. Even more seriously, our lives will lack integrity. Outwardly, we will need to project confidence, spiritual and emotional health and wholeness, while inwardly we may be filled with self-doubts, anxieties, self-pity, and old grudges.[6]

As followers of Jesus who are looking to experience deep soul transformation, let us prioritize our time to focus on the inner self. Let us be still and let God speak to us in the quiet. Let us enter into the space of serenity where the presence of God will meet us. In this space, we will experience a restfulness that will give us great assurance that God is at work in our lives. Let us take all of who we are into the still and quiet presence of God. There we will encounter something majestic.

---

5. Foster, *Celebration of Discipline*, 86.
6. Keller, *Prayer*, 22.

Prayer

There are so many things that can be said about prayer, but I believe that prayer is the power source of connecting with God. Prayer is intentional communication with the Creator of the universe. In prayer, we encounter the peace and presence of God. When Paul was writing his letter to the church in Philippi, he wrote, "Don't worry about anything, but in everything, through prayer and petition with thanksgiving, present your requests to God. And the peace of God, which surpasses all understanding, will guard your hearts and minds in Christ Jesus" (Phil 4:6–7). In prayer, we are met with the peace of God. Whether or not we understand what is going on in our lives, when we find ourselves uncertain when it comes to making big decisions, when we simply need clarity in our lives, or when we just need to meet with God—prayer will unify us with the heart of God. As kingdom people who will spend eternity in the presence of God, we must do our part in pursuing God by communicating with him through prayer. There is an immense amount of transformation in our souls when we become a people of prayer. When we pray, we are not the same. Prayer opens us up into a vulnerable state, as we cast our cares upon the Lord, trusting that he will meet us exactly where we are at. We are to come as we are and trust that Jesus is going to transform us according to his plan and purpose for our lives. Paul Miller, in his book *A Praying Life*, writes this:

> *Prayer opens us up into a vulnerable state, as we cast our cares upon the Lord, trusting that he will meet us exactly where we are at.*

> Jesus wants us to be without pretense when we come to him in prayer. Instead, we often try to be something we aren't. We begin by concentrating on God, but almost immediately our minds wander off in a dozen different directions. The problems of the day push out our well-intentioned resolve to be spiritual. We give ourselves a spiritual kick in the pants and try again, but life crowds out prayer. We know that prayer isn't supposed to be like this, so we give up in despair. We might as well get something done. What's the problem? We're trying to be spiritual, to get it right. We know we don't need to clean up our act in order to become Christian, but when it comes to praying, we forget that. We, like adults, try to fix ourselves up. In contrast, Jesus wants us to come to him like

little children, just as we are. The difficulty of coming just as we are is that we are messy. And prayer makes it worse. When we slow down to pray, we are immediately confronted with how unspiritual we are, with how difficult it is to concentrate on God. We don't know how bad we are until we try to be good. Nothing exposes our selfishness and spiritual powerlessness like prayer.[7]

What Miller reveals is that we are all broken. When we come to prayer, we ought not to assume that our lives are all put together and that we need to deliver a cookie-cutter prayer to the God who knows our hearts. Prayer is essential in that it reveals just how broken we are. If we are willing to be real and authentic in prayer, we will see just how powerful, perfect, holy, and incredible our God is. Our imperfection and brokenness are the perfect formula for God to work with. It is in our imperfection and brokenness that God can bring restoration and healing to our lives. Let us not pretend like we are put together. Let us freely, willingly, and openly voice our genuine hearts in prayer before a God who is tender, compassionate, and forgiving. God will meet us in the spiritual rhythm of prayer. We will encounter the powerful presence of God through prayer when we anticipate the Holy Spirit to intercede and clash with our utterances. When we grant God access to the dwelling place of the Holy Spirit in our lives—that is, our bodies—the presence of God will come and reside in our very being, bringing us comfort, peace, sustenance, and nourishment, which ultimately leads to our spiritual vitality. Prayer can be difficult for so many people, but that is why it is important to just pray.

There is power in going to the feet of Jesus feeling empty and drained. It is when we are empty and drained that the Spirit of the living God infuses our souls and quenches our thirst. We are powerless. We are empty. We long to be filled with the presence of God. Early on in our prayer lives, we may begin to recognize that we have nothing to give—we are spiritually empty. The great Tim Keller does a great job articulating the tension of the praying life. Keller writes:

> The first thing we learn in attempting to pray is our spiritual emptiness—and this lesson is crucial. We are so used to being empty that we do not recognize the emptiness as such until we start to try to pray. We don't feel it until we begin to read what the Bible and others have said about the greatness and promise of prayer. Then

---

7. Miller, *Praying Life*, 30–31.

we finally begin to feel lonely and hungry. It's an important first step to fellowship with God.[8]

Keller goes on:

> When your prayer life finally begins to flourish, the effects can be remarkable. You may be filled with self-pity, and be justifying resentment and anger. Then you sit down to pray and the reorientation that comes before God's face reveals the pettiness of your feelings in an instant. All your self-justifying excuses fall to the ground in pieces. Or you may be filled with anxiety, and during prayer you come to wonder what you were so worried about. You laugh at yourself and thank God for who he is and what he's done. It can be that dramatic. It is the bracing clarity of a new perspective. Eventually, this can be a normal experience, but that is never how the prayer life starts. In the beginning the feeling of poverty and absence usually dominate, but the best guides for this phase urge us not to turn back but rather to endure and pray in a disciplined way, until, as Packer and Nostrum say, we get through duty to delight.[9]

There is so much in these powerful words from Tim Keller. I believe the biggest takeaway is that prayer is a process. In prayer, we wrestle and plea while being expectant and anticipatory for God to move in our hearts. We are invited to come as we are, and God will come as he is. He is not surprised by our requests. He is not surprised by our pleas. He is not surprised by our anger and frustration. He welcomes it all. So let us go to the Father of glory with vulnerable hearts and open minds, giving him room to give us a kingdom heart while transforming us for life on earth as it is in heaven. Prayer is an invitation from God to participate in the alignment of his will for us. As Keller puts it, "Prayer is awe, intimacy, struggle—yet the way to reality. There is nothing more important, or harder, or richer, or more life-altering. There is absolutely nothing so great as prayer."[10] Let us pray.

> Prayer is an invitation from God to participate in the alignment of his will for us.

---

8. Keller, *Prayer*, 24–25.
9. Keller, *Prayer*, 24–25.
10. Keller, *Prayer*, 32.

Fasting

I like to eat. A lot. I am a self-proclaimed foodie. Whenever my wife and I travel, much of our plans include where we are going to eat. We like to try everything, from different ethnic foods to having a good ole American pub burger. A lot of our lives revolve around food. Traditionally, when we are called to fast, many of us abstain from food. This spiritual practice intends for us to abstain from food for the sake of focusing on God. I have always viewed this spiritual practice in a way that replaces my hunger for a meal with my hunger for God. Instead of focusing my attention on the food that I am going to eat, I focus my attention on the God I get to serve. So anytime my stomach begins to rumble, I can't help but stop and pray. When there is a desire to eat, we ought to fill that desire and longing for the Holy Spirit to permeate our lives. We must be aware that when we attempt to give everything we are to the cause of obtaining spiritual nourishment through fasting, the enemy will attempt to intervene in these plans and find a way to disorient us.

Fasting is a discipline that many in Bible times practiced. When Israel rebelled, Moses felt compelled to fast. Moses writes:

> I fell down like the first time in the presence of the Lord for forty days and forty nights; I did not eat food or drink water because of all the sin you committed, doing what was evil in the Lord's sight and angering him. I was afraid of the fierce anger the Lord had directed against you, because he was about to destroy you. But again the Lord listened to me on that occasion. (Deut 9:18–19)

Because of Israel's rebellion and the worship of idols, Moses felt the urge to fast on behalf of the rebellious people. Israel had breached God's covenant, and Moses sought to bring mending and restoration for this rebellion. Fasting is a powerful spiritual rhythm for when we seek to intercede on behalf of others so that the work of God can be experienced. I had a friend once who had to make a massive, life-altering decision, and I committed to fasting, along with a handful of others, so that God would bring clarity to the situation. When we fast, we invite God to give us wisdom for minor or major decisions in our lives. Moses knew this. So Moses stepped up and interceded on behalf of the Israelite people. As mentioned in the Scripture portion of this section on spiritual rhythms, Jesus fasted right before entering into the wilderness (Matt 4:1–11). We must consider fasting so that we can grow in our spiritual vitality.

When it comes to our attempt to fast we must remember that fasting does not always mean taking a break from food. To fast simply means to abstain from something, and commonly, abstaining from food was a great practice to depend on and connect with God. But food does not have to be the only source of fasting. We can choose to abstain from social media, television, our cell phones, spending money, coffee (which seems pretty impossible to me as I live with coffee in my veins at all times), and anything else you can think of that you can replace or abstain from while you focus on giving that energy over to God. The entire goal of fasting is to set aside something that calls for our attention that can be omitted for the sake of growing deeper in our knowledge and intimacy with God. Perhaps it is food, because we all get hungry throughout the day. When we desire to consume and digest food, we can replace those desires with the consumption of God and his presence. He will fill us up and satisfy our souls.

Sabbath

Living in America, there is just no time for the Sabbath. There is no time for me to talk about the Sabbath, so let us move on . . . I'm joking, of course. The Sabbath day essentially means that there is an abstaining from work. In the creation account, we see God taking time to create the earth and everything that is in it (Gen 1:1–31). After the completion of his creation, God rests (Gen 2:2). The creation account puts it this way, "So the heavens and the earth and everything in them were completed. On the seventh day God had completed his work that he had done, and he rested on the seventh day from all the work that he had done. God blessed the seventh day and declared it holy, for on it he rested from all his work of creation" (Gen 2:1–3). The *Faithlife Study Bible* puts it this way, "The Hebrew verb used here, *shavath*, means 'cease' or 'rest.' The English word 'Sabbath' comes from the related Hebrew noun *shabbath*. The word implies that God's work of creation was completed, so He stopped."[11] The work of God was finished, and God's response to this was rest. This day was made holy, set apart (Gen 2:3). It was different. It was unlike any other day that God had made.

The Sabbath can be intimidating, because we simply do not have time to rest. There is always something that needs to be done. As with anything in Scripture, we can tend to treat the Sabbath in a legalistic vein. That is not why God created the Sabbath. The Sabbath is not intended to bind us up

---

11. Barry et al., *Faithlife Study Bible*, Gen 2:2.

and make us feel like if we don't sabbath on the seventh day, God is going to be mad at us. Even more so, the Sabbath does not have to be Sunday. Many people treat Sunday as their Sabbath day and believe that is the Holy Day. Sunday is indeed special in that most people attend church on Sunday for worship gatherings across the globe, but not everyone can make Sunday their Sabbath. For example, I am a pastor. Sundays do not feel like a day that I can rest. I am up way early in the morning. I get to church around six to seven in the morning. I read, pray, and prepare the final touches on my sermon for that day. I exert much of my introverted energy as I become an extrovert for a couple of hours. I worship with our church family, I preach, and then I continue to dialogue with people in conversations. By the time everyone leaves, the church gets locked up, and I get home, I am fried. Sunday was not a day of rest. It was set apart in that I went to church and gathered with fellow brothers and sisters in Christ for worship, but it was far from restful as a full-time pastor. Sundays cannot be my Sabbath. I take Fridays off so that I can rest and recover from a long, mentally taxing, and physically draining workweek. My Sabbath is on Friday. For others, it's Saturday. For others, it's Monday. It is good to have a day that we set apart for rest, relaxation, and rejuvenation. There is a reason that every one of us needs sleep each night (unless you are nocturnal). Our bodies were not meant to plow through the trenches twenty-four-seven. We need breaks in our days to sleep and recover, so that we can press on the next day.

I believe that this was God's intent when it came to the Sabbath. God knew that we would be working and toiling. It gets exhausting, and we need to recover—so we rest. When we don't intentionally take the Sabbath, we are declaring that our to-do lists are more important than God's. Not taking a Sabbath refuses God's good gift to his people. We must be renewed and refreshed. It is in the renewal and refreshment of a Sabbath that we can take a deep breath and keep going. Again, the Sabbath is not meant to be a legalistic action item. The Sabbath is a special and unique opportunity to enjoy what God created for his people. The Scripture gives us an example of what Sabbath legalism can lead to and what Sabbath freedom is meant for. The Gospel writer Mark records this:

> *When we don't intentionally take the Sabbath, we are declaring that our to-do lists are more important than God's.*

> On the Sabbath he [Jesus] was going through the grainfields, and his disciples began to make their way, picking some heads of grain. The Pharisees said to him, "Look, why are they doing what is not lawful on the Sabbath?" He said to them, "Have you never read what David and those who were with him did when he was in need and hungry—how he entered the house of God in the time of Abiathar the high priest and ate the bread of the Presence—which is not lawful for anyone to eat except the priests—and also gave some to his companions?" Then he told them, "The Sabbath was made for man and not man for the Sabbath. So then, the Son of Man is Lord even of the Sabbath." (Mark 2:23–28)

Jesus is extremely witty and clever. The Pharisees—who were a people of the law—would frequently seek opportunities to catch Jesus doing something unlawful, or against the law, and would attempt to make plans to bring him down (Luke 6:6–11). They would gossip among themselves, being filled with self-righteousness. Their legalism is something that Jesus would frequently disassemble and show them a new way. So when it came to walking through the grainfields, while Jesus's disciples would pick the heads of grain, the Pharisees became furious. How could someone not set apart the one, literal Sabbath day? Jesus used this opportunity as a teachable moment. He noticed that the Pharisees were trying to pin him and his disciples. So Jesus used an illustration:

> "Have you never read what David and those who were with him did when he was in need and hungry—how he entered the house of God in the time of Abiathar the high priest and ate the bread of the Presence—which is not lawful for anyone to eat except the priests—and also gave some to his companions?" Then he told them, "The Sabbath was made for man and not man for the Sabbath. So then, the Son of Man is Lord even of the Sabbath." (Mark 2:25–28)

The Pharisees thought that Jesus was disobeying the duty of taking the Sabbath literally, and Jesus reframed the entire purpose of the Sabbath. Jesus said that the Sabbath was made for man and not man for the Sabbath. The *Faithlife Study Bible* parses this out by stating, "This enigmatic statement likely means that the Sabbath was established to give people rest. The Pharisees' overzealous protection of the Sabbath has lost sight of its purpose and turned it into something burdensome."[12] The Sabbath ought not to be

---

12. Barry et al., *Faithlife Study Bible*, Mark 2:27.

burdensome. The Sabbath is not something we do because we have to; it is something we do because we get to. The Sabbath was made for humanity to enjoy. It is yet another gift that is given by God to humanity. Our bodies are fragile and need to rest to recover. In the busyness of our lives, let us receive and enjoy the beautiful gift of the Sabbath. Let us not be consumed by the pressures of keeping up with the speed of the world around us, and let us take an intentional day to pause and reflect on the goodness of our God.

Reflection and Meditation

I once watched a segment on TV where people who were in their eighties and nineties were asked about their biggest regrets in life. The common answer that kept coming up was that they had wished they had spent more time reflecting. People who know me know that I can sometimes be an old man. One of the things that makes me an old man is that I love to sit still in the wilderness and simply reflect. Reflecting on the things in life is one of my favorite pastimes.

Reflection and mediation are spiritual rhythms that allow us to recollect and reminisce on who God is and what God has done and has been doing in our lives. Meditation is a thought practice that allows us to think about the things of God. Meditation is especially powerful when we meditate on the Scriptures. If you recall, the Lord spoke to Joshua after the death of Moses and commissioned him with a powerful charge. The Lord said:

> No one will be able to stand against you as long as you live. I will be with you, just as I was with Moses. I will not leave you or abandon you. Be strong and courageous, for you will distribute the land I swore to their ancestors to give them as an inheritance. Above all, be strong and very courageous to observe carefully the whole instruction my servant Moses commanded you. Do not turn from it to the right or the left, so that you will have success wherever you go. (Josh 1:5–7)

This encouragement from the Lord is enough to pause, reflect, and meditate on. It shows God's faithfulness to his people. It shows that God cares and has a purpose for Joshua's life. But following this charge to Joshua, God gave special instruction to Joshua: "This book of instruction must not depart from your mouth; you are to meditate on it day and night so that you may carefully observe everything written in it. For then you will prosper and succeed in whatever you do" (Josh 1:8). It is likely that the book of instruction that God was alluding to included the laws of Deuteronomy. Meditating on these laws would allow Joshua to lead the people well. He would be able to have his thoughts renewed by the law that was given by God. This would cleanse and purify Joshua's thought life for the betterment of his leadership.

It is vital for our spiritual formation that we purify our thought life. When we don't do this, our minds can be filled with fear, anxiety, worry, despair, hate, and annoyance—to name just a few. But when we invite the Holy Spirit into our thought life, God can cleanse our minds so that our minds can be renewed and refreshed with a kingdom mindset. Paul writes to the church in Rome, "Do not be conformed to this age, but be transformed by the renewing of your mind, so that you may discern what is the good, pleasing, and perfect will of God" (Rom 12:2). Our spiritual vitality prospers when we spend quality time meditating on the riches of God and his word. The psalmist writes, "How happy is the one who does not walk in the advice of the wicked or stand in the pathway with sinners or sit in the company of mockers! Instead, his delight is in the Lord's instruction, and he meditates on it day and night. He is like a tree planted beside flowing streams that bears its fruit in its season, and its leaf does not wither. Whatever he does prospers" (Ps 1:1–3). Let us be people who meditate on God and his ways so that we may draw ever nearer to him (Ps 119:15). Let us reflect on God's goodness and faithfulness toward his people. As Ps 105 reminds us:

> Give thanks to the Lord, call on his name;
>   proclaim his deeds among the peoples.
> Sing to him, sing praise to him;
>   tell about all his wondrous works!
> Boast in his holy name;
>   let the hearts of those who seek the Lord rejoice.
> Seek the Lord and his strength;
>   seek his face always.
> Remember the wondrous works he has done,
>   his wonders, and the judgments he has pronounced,
> you offspring of Abraham his servant,
>   Jacob's descendants—his chosen ones. (Ps 105:1–6)

This praise psalm recounts the incredible work of Yahweh. The psalmist here declares the majesty and wonder of our great God. Let us, too, be reminded of the goodness of our God and be intentional in seeking him, while reflecting and meditating on his goodness.

Service

Serving God and serving others is a powerful way to experience the presence of God. The church I currently pastor recently did an initiative that was called Faith in Action Sunday. Faith in Action Sunday was an intentional step to go outside the walls of our local church body and enter into the spaces of the community. Team leaders took teams all over the community to serve the people in the city however they could. It was simply about laying ourselves down for the sake of caring for the needs of the community.

There is something profound when followers of Jesus come together for the cause of serving others. The spiritual rhythm of service is rooted in what the Gospel writer Mark said about Jesus himself: "For even the Son of Man did not come to be served, but to serve, and to give his life as a ransom for many" (Mark 10:45). Though Jesus was indeed served, this is not why he came. Jesus came to serve and ultimately give his life as a ransom for many. This was accomplished throughout Jesus's life and ministry and what was displayed on a criminal's cross. Jesus spent his life putting the needs of others first. He sacrificially served people throughout the New Testament. Everything from feeding the five thousand (Matt 14:13–21) to his sacrificial death on the cross to save humanity from sin (Matt 27:32–56). The whole of Christ's life was centered on serving others. R. A. Cole writes, "This is an argument of the 'how much more' type, often used by Jesus in the gospels. Even Jesus came not to enjoy the service of others, but to accept a lowly servant's place: how much more his servants! But he also came *to give his life as a ransom for many*."[13] If there is anything that we can learn from Jesus, it is that he gave his life so that others would live.

As followers of Jesus, we must be compelled to serve the kingdom of God by serving others. We must consider those around us. Those who are in less fortunate situations than us. Those who don't have much. Those who are in our congregations, communities, and the world. Our impulse to serve others reveals our spiritual temperature. When our spiritual temperature is boiling, we will instinctively consider the needs of others before our own. Jesus always considered the needs of others. Specifically, serving others was the very heart of who Jesus was. In the Gospel of John, Jesus washed his disciple's feet (John 13:1–11). He would later explain the significance of foot washing:

> When Jesus had washed their feet and put on his outer clothing, he reclined again and said to them, "Do you know what I have

---

13. Cole, *Mark*, 248.

> done for you? You call me Teacher and Lord—and you are speaking rightly, since that is what I am. So if I, your Lord and Teacher, have washed your feet, you also ought to wash one another's feet. For I have given you an example, that you also should do just as I have done for you. "Truly I tell you, a servant is not greater than his master, and a messenger is not greater than the one who sent him. If you know these things, you are blessed if you do them." (John 13:12–20)

When Jesus washed his disciple's feet, he modeled humility and servanthood. These modeled a compassionate heart and a compassionate mind that Jesus would frequently display. I don't know about you, but I think that feet are disgusting. They are smelly and gross. But when we consider the feet of the disciples, those must have been seriously dirty because they would often walk barefoot everywhere they went. Jesus's act of servanthood and humility was a demonstration of how we ought to serve and care for one another. We must make ourselves lowly. Jesus must increase, and we must decrease (John 3:30). We magnify the name of Jesus when we become lower than our neighbors. This posture develops our spiritual vitality and prepares us for what kingdom life on earth looks like. The apostle Paul did an outstanding job writing about the power of humility—specifically looking at the person of Jesus:

> Do nothing out of selfish ambition or conceit, but in humility consider others as more important than yourselves. Everyone should look not to his own interests, but rather to the interests of others. Adopt the same attitude as that of Christ Jesus, who, existing in the form of God, did not consider equality with God as something to be exploited. Instead he emptied himself by assuming the form of a servant, taking on the likeness of humanity. And when he had come as a man, he humbled himself by becoming obedient to the point of death—even to death on a cross. For this reason God highly exalted him and gave him the name that is above every name, so that at the name of Jesus every knee will bow—in heaven and on earth and under the earth—and every tongue will confess that Jesus Christ is Lord, to the glory of God the Father. (Phil 2:3–11)

What if this was our heartbeat? What if we did nothing out of selfish ambition or conceit? How much greater would our lives demonstrate the life of Christ if we, in humility, considered others as more important than ourselves? Our lives would resemble the life of Jesus. Jesus put the needs of others before his own. Jesus always cared for and demonstrated compassion for those around him. Even those who were considered his enemies. Let us consider others before ourselves. Let us serve people with a heart of humility. Let us ask God to give us the strength to love and care about others—including those we consider our opposition or enemies. Our sinful nature makes us enemies with God. But through the blood of Jesus, we are made new and redeemed. Jesus cared for us so much that he willingly laid down his life for us. Let us give our lives for the sake of the gospel. Let us offer ourselves and serve our friends, our enemies, our neighbors, our communities, and our churches. When we do, we will see God at work.

Worship as Lifestyle

We have addressed the spiritual rhythm of worship several times throughout this book. But this spiritual rhythm is extremely important when it comes to us living life on earth as it is in heaven. Worship is a lifestyle. It is something that is part of who we are. We were all created to worship. Due to the fall of humanity and the potency of sin and its entrance into the world, humanity chooses to worship many things besides God. Our worship experience is deterred by a world that wants our worship. So we naturally are inclined to pursue the many things in life, putting God on the back burner. Worship is where desire and worth cross in life. So when we consider what we deem worthy—what comes to mind? Is God our first thought? Or do other things come to mind when we think of that which is worthy?

Since we were created for worship, we must intentionally alter our thinking and our mindset to worship God and God alone. This practice stems from the spiritual rhythm of reflection and meditation. Our thought life is vital in the wholeness of how we operate. So if we are aiming to operate toward the end goal of worshiping God above all else, we must renew our minds to communicate to our hearts that we are longing to worship God.

In Matthew's Gospel, when the Pharisees asked Jesus what the greatest command was, Jesus replied, "Love the Lord your God with all your heart, with all your soul, and with all your mind" (Matt 22:37). This kind of love that Jesus requires of us is a love that is all in. It's not just an intellectual love. It's not just an emotional love. It's not just a love that comes from within. It's all of these things coming together into one. Worship, just like love, requires all our heart, all our soul, and all our mind. This makes up the whole of who we are and what we have to offer. When we come to worship, we come with our all. Worship requires us to set aside the desires we have to fully desire the presence of God. Psalm 95 gives us a wonderful glimpse into what authentic worship can look like:

> Come, let's shout joyfully to the Lord,
>   shout triumphantly to the rock of our salvation!
> Let's enter his presence with thanksgiving;
>   let's shout triumphantly to him in song.
> For the Lord is a great God,
>   a great King above all gods.
> The depths of the earth are in his hand,
>   and the mountain peaks are his.
> The sea is his; he made it.
>   His hands formed the dry land.
> Come, let's worship and bow down;
>   let's kneel before the Lord our Maker. (Ps 95:1–6)

The psalmist begins with an invitation to worship by saying, "Come." In worship, we are to come. We approach the Lord, and because we enter into his presence, we can shout joyfully to him. This does not mean that when we come to worship we must be happy. Life has its ups and downs. We face trials and hardships, which can make for many difficulties. The beauty of who God is, is that even when we are facing difficulties in life, we can approach the throne of grace and experience joy in our hearts when we come to him in worship. God welcomes us just as we are when we come to him and meets us in our circumstances, assuring us of his goodness and grace over our lives. We must strive to enter into the courts of praise by coming just as we are and not who we think we are supposed to be. When we are our authentic selves, God will meet with us, he will nourish us, and he will rejuvenate us. If you are thirsty, come and drink of the deep well of grace and be satisfied.

Community

Community with others can be an intimidating thing. In a community we welcome others into our lives, sharing ourselves with those around us. This is certainly a challenge for many—especially if one is introverted (like myself). Doing life with people requires trust. If we don't trust someone, then doing community with them can be a challenge. Many people resist life together because of previous experiences, personal reservations, past hurt, a shy personality, or simply having a difficult time sharing their life with someone. There is no shame in any of these. The pain that people face certainly impacts the way they interact with others. This should not be taken lightly. If you are someone who has been wounded by others—especially in the church—do not give up on life together. Seek help. Seek restoration. Seek healing. Life in a community enables us to participate in life together. We are not called to do this thing called life on our own. Yes, as we mentioned earlier, solitude is very important to recharge, but we cannot suppress life together as followers of Jesus. The kingdom will be filled with people, and we will always do life alongside other believers, forevermore. Now is the time to practice and prepare for an eternity with others. One of my favorite Bible passages (which has been used in this book already) is Acts 2:42–47.

In this early section of Acts, Luke gives us a powerful version of what the early church community looked like. I want to take a look at Acts 2:42 for a moment. Luke writes, "They devoted themselves to the apostles' teaching, to the fellowship, to the breaking of bread, and to prayer" (Acts 2:42). The word "they" here refers to followers of Jesus. These are new converts who gave their lives over to Christ. After giving their lives to Jesus, they committed themselves to four crucial practices: the apostles' teaching, fellowship, the breaking of bread, and prayer. Regarding the apostles' teaching, one commentator put it this way, "First, there was the *teaching* given by the *apostles*, who were qualified for this task by their companionship with Jesus."[14] Those who were close to Jesus and knew the things that he taught were able to share those teachings with all who were involved in the early Christian church. This unified the church. Their devotion was to be centered and rooted in the things that Jesus taught. This brought unity to the community. They shared in the common experience of what it means to follow Jesus and devote their lives to him. That was enough for them to say, "I'm in." The Holy Spirit was on the move and would speak through people so that people were encouraged, inspired, equipped, convicted, and unified. The Holy Spirit came on the scene, and people were confused (Acts 2:14–15). Then, Peter gave an exhortation that was rooted in what the prophet Joel had said:

> And it will be in the last days, says God, that I will pour out my Spirit on all people; then your sons and your daughters will prophesy, your young men will see visions, and your old men will dream

---

14. Marshall, *Acts*, 88 (emphases original).

dreams. I will even pour out my Spirit on my servants in those days, both men and women and they will prophesy. I will display wonders in the heaven above and signs on the earth below: blood and fire and a cloud of smoke. The sun will be turned to darkness and the moon to blood before the great and glorious day of the Lord comes. Then everyone who calls on the name of the Lord will be saved. (Acts 2:17–21)

The presence of the Holy Spirit that came upon the people in Acts was the fulfillment of a prophecy. Not only was this a fulfillment of Joel's prophecy, but this prophecy suggested that sons and daughters would prophesy. This word "prophecy" in Greek is *prophēteuō*, meaning "under like prompting, to teach, refute, reprove, admonish, comfort others."[15] Sons and daughters (humankind) would be the mouthpieces that God would use to articulate and communicate his word to the world. So as believers gathered in Acts 2:42, we see this being fleshed out. There is a commitment to God and his word as they seek to sit under the apostles' teaching. This community demonstrates their commitment to God and his word. They are fed, filled up, and nourished. After first committing themselves to devotion to God's word, we see followers of Jesus growing in their relationships with one another.

Luke writes in Acts 2:42 that the followers of Jesus devoted themselves to the fellowship. The Greek word for "fellowship" is *koinōnia*, which can be translated as "association, community, communion, joint participation" or "the share which one has in anything."[16] In layman's terms, *koinōnia* means life together. So as these early followers of Jesus were growing in their faith walk with the Lord, they were also committed to simply doing life together. These believers were committed to partnering together and participating in community with one another. Individuals may grow in their spiritual formation through their personal development, but their spiritual formation cannot be experienced to the fullest apart from community. After all, God created people for one another. All of humanity embodies the image-bearing nature of God (Gen 1:27). From the very beginning, God had the intent of creating humanity in his image. This image reflected who God is in his Triune nature—Father, Son, and Holy Spirit. Referring to this passage, the *Faithlife Study Bible* suggests, "The occurrence of 'us' in this passage has been understood to refer to the plurality of the godhead: the Father,

---

15. See https://www.blueletterbible.org/lexicon/g4395/csb/tr/0-1/.
16. See https://www.blueletterbible.org/lexicon/g2842/csb/tr/0-1/.

Son, and Holy Spirit."[17] What this reveals about God is that he functions in community within the Trinity. As image-bearers of God, human beings best reflect the image of God when they are living in community with one another. It is in community that Christians are made to look more like their Creator. Christians can learn to love one another in the context of community—regardless of their similarities or differences. Christians can bear one another's burdens in the context of community (Gal 6:2). Christians can keep one another accountable in the context of community (Prov 27:27). Christians can intercede on behalf of one another in the community. As the great theologian Dietrich Bonhoeffer writes, "A Christian fellowship lives and exists by the intercession of its members for one another, or it collapses."[18] Believers need one another for the growth and preservation of their spiritual formation. God has always been at work among his people. When the people of God gather together, God shows up in ways that give people the opportunity to grow and experience community with one another. It is in these communities that people grow in their spiritual formation. And ultimately, we encounter kingdom presence through sharing in one another's presence.

EXPERIENCING KINGDOM PRESENCE

> *If we want to experience the presence of God, we must do our part in pursuing that experience.*

We have spent this chapter looking at the ways that we can experience kingdom presence on earth as it is in heaven. If we want to experience the presence of God, we must do our part in pursuing that experience. God is faithful, living, and active in our lives. He desires that we notice him and prioritize him in our lives. He loves us and wants to spend time with us. When we take the step forward to encountering the presence of God, we will not be the same. We will be forever changed. Experiencing the kingdom on earth means that we lean into spiritual rhythms that will usher us into the presence of God. Spiritual rhythms such as Scripture reading, spending time in solitude, praying, fasting, taking the Sabbath and keeping it holy, reflecting and meditation, serving, developing a worship lifestyle, and pursuing intentional community. When we commit ourselves

---

17. Barry et al., *Faithlife Study Bible*, Gen 1:26.
18. Bonhoeffer, *Life Together*, 65.

to interacting with these spiritual rhythms, we will find that God will meet us there.

PROCESS AND REFLECT: KINGDOM PRESENCE

1. When you think of the presence of God, what comes to mind?
2. How do you encounter the presence of God in your life?
3. Have you ever felt like God has been far from you, which caused you to doubt God? How did you respond, and how did you grow from that situation? If you haven't, what advice can you give others?
4. What spiritual rhythm do you excel in the most? How did this come to be?
5. What spiritual rhythm do you excel in the least? What do you think causes this?

CHAPTER 6

Kingdom Spirit

And I will ask the Father, and he will give you another Counselor to be with you forever. He is the Spirit of truth. The world is unable to receive him because it doesn't see him or know him. But you do know him, because he remains with you and will be in you.

—John 14:16–18

I'm not a handyman. Far from it, actually. If you need me to fix something, I will only give you a reason to never ask me again. My dad is a jack-of-all-trades. He can fix almost anything that anyone may need help with. Professionally, he is a general contractor, so that helps. I was having some plumbing issues with my kitchen sink. Some of the piping was disassembled. I had no clue how to fix the problem—at all. Something needed to be done. So I went into my garage, found some lumber, and screwed a bunch of wood together. I used it to prop up one of the pipes so it would be loose. It worked! Well, it worked temporarily. A few weeks later, water began to leak again. My parents were visiting us one weekend, and I mentioned to my dad the issues that we were having in my kitchen. So he went to the store, purchased the necessary pieces, and fixed the plumbing issue. His help was everything that I needed. I called on him, and he came through. He assisted me, and he was there to provide the tools needed to fix the plumbing issue. Though I didn't want to admit it at first, I did need assistance.

Just like in our personal lives, our spiritual lives need assistance. We were never meant to walk with Jesus alone. As we talked about previously, we all need community with other followers of Jesus. This will strengthen our faith journey and surround our lives with people who we can do life with. But we also need assistance daily, hourly, and assistance on a moment-by-moment basis. Simply put, we need ongoing aid from a higher power. Praise be to God that we have a solution! God gave us the incredible gift of having a Counselor, an advocate, who resides within our very being. This gift is the gift of the Holy Spirit. If we are going to live our lives on earth as it is in heaven, we are going to need help from the Holy Spirit of God to lead and guide us moment by moment.

A statement made by Jesus in the Gospel of John was revolutionary. It was life changing for the disciples, for believers, and for all who would come thereafter. Jesus knew that his time on earth was coming to an end. He was aware of the days that he had left before his gruesome crucifixion. In the flesh, Jesus was able to be present with only a certain amount of people. The promise he made to the disciples would change the trajectory of human history. Jesus said to them, "I will ask the Father, and he will give you another Counselor to be with you forever. He is the Spirit of truth. The world is unable to receive him because it doesn't see him or know him. But you do know him, because he remains with you and will be in you" (John 14:16–18). This could have easily startled the disciples. Where was Jesus going? Who was he sending to them? Would this Counselor truly live *in* them? One commentator explains it this way:

> What did Jesus mean when he said the Counsellor will be "in you"? The words the NIV translates as "in you" (*en hymin*) may also be rendered "among you," seeing that the pronoun "you" here is plural. However, just a few verses later, Jesus individualized this promise when he said (when the Spirit comes) the Father and the Son would make their home with the individual believer (21–23). In the light of this later statement it is best to interpret the promise that the Counsellor will "be in you" to include an indwelling of individual believers as well as his presence among them as a group.[1]

What a powerful exposition of the text by Colin Kruse. I believe Colin is spot on when considering this Counselor. There is a literal indwelling for the believer when Jesus is part of their life. Jesus indwells the believer's temple, or body, when their faith is placed in him. This is the message that

---

1. Kruse, *John*, 302–3.

Jesus tried to get across to his disciples. He is leaving them physically, but he will indwell them by way of the Spirit of God.

When we flip forward in the New Testament, we see an interaction with Jesus and his disciples yet again. Luke, the author of Acts, records this:

> While he was with them, he commanded them not to leave Jerusalem, but to wait for the Father's promise. "Which," he said, "you have heard me speak about; for John baptized with water, but you will be baptized with the Holy Spirit in a few days." So when they had come together, they asked him, "Lord, are you restoring the kingdom to Israel at this time?" He said to them, "It is not for you to know times or periods that the Father has set by his own authority. But you will receive power when the Holy Spirit has come on you, and you will be my witnesses in Jerusalem, in all Judea and Samaria, and to the ends of the earth." (Acts 1:4–8)

The once-promised Holy Spirit was preparing to arrive on the scene. The disciples would be empowered and equipped to multiply the gospel in their local context and abroad. Not on their own accord but by the power of the Holy Spirit. After informing his disciples of the Holy Spirit, Jesus ascended into heaven (Acts 1:9).

When the day of Pentecost arrived, the Holy Spirit finally made its way into the lives of Jesus's followers. Luke writes this:

> When the day of Pentecost had arrived, they were all together in one place. Suddenly a sound like that of a violent rushing wind came from heaven, and it filled the whole house where they were staying. They saw tongues like flames of fire that separated and rested on each one of them. Then they were all filled with the Holy Spirit and began to speak in different tongues, as the Spirit enabled them. (Acts 2:1–4)

What a crazy thing to experience. The Spirit of the living God came in like a violent, rushing wind. The Spirit filled the whole house, and they experienced things unlike ever before. This is how the Spirit of God entered into the presence of believers at first. The Spirit enabled believers to do things that they had never done before. The promise that Jesus had made earlier on was coming to fruition. Everything was changing. But God was on the move. There was power in the Spirit of the living God simply through the

> The Spirit enabled believers to do things that they had never done before.

Spirit's presence. Just like the prophet Joel had prophesied, it had come to be: "And it will be in the last days, says God, that I will pour out my Spirit on all people; then your sons and your daughters will prophesy, your young men will see visions, and your old men will dream dreams. I will even pour out my Spirit on my servants in those days, both men and women and they will prophesy" (Acts 2:17–18). This is what Peter preached when the Holy Spirit came on the scene (Acts 2:14–41). The message of the gospel would not be contained. It was going to spread like wildfire, and the Holy Spirit was making it all possible. Followers of Jesus—both sons and daughters of King Jesus—would bear the good news and be the vessels by which God would speak his word. The Spirit of God enabled followers of Jesus to be good-news people—kingdom people—who were led by the Holy Spirit.

> The Spirit of the living God equips, empowers, and enables followers of Jesus to have the necessary strength to face the challenges of life.

The Spirit reveals the person of Jesus to people so that lives can be transformed. The Spirit of the living God equips, empowers, and enables followers of Jesus to have the necessary strength to face the challenges of life. Life is difficult and has many highs and lows—ups and downs. But we are not alone in carrying the burdens in our lives. The presence of God pours out on us through the Holy Spirit, filling us with the sustenance that we need to get through. The God who made the universe come into existence, who walked this earth in human flesh, is the same God that dwells within us by way of the Holy Spirit. Think about how powerful that is! When we don't have what it takes to get through another day, the Spirit of God will aid us with all that we need to get through. When we can't muster up the courage to step out in faith in something that we feel called to, the Spirit of God will enable us with the power to take a leap of faith and trust in God. When we need guidance and direction, the Spirit of God will lead and guide us to where God desires us to go. When we struggle to love our neighbors—especially those who think, look, and act differently than us—the Spirit of God will give us the ability to love others well. Many of these things we cannot do on our own. We need help. That is why the Spirit of God is our Counselor (John 14:16). The Spirit is our Helper and our Advocate. As kingdom people, we have the opportunity to experience this promised indwelling. When we give our lives over to Jesus and become his followers, we can experience Christ Jesus in our very selves, as our bodies are the temple for the Holy Spirit to reside within. As kingdom people—who hope to live life on earth as it is in heaven, let us long for the Spirit of the living God to be our Guide, Comforter, Source of peace, and Advocate. The more we are in tune with the Spirit in our lives, the more our lives will resemble a kingdom life on earth.

WE ARE AMBASSADORS

Not that long ago, I found out that I could buy shares in my favorite soccer team, Manchester United. That's right. I could become a very partial owner of a professional sports team and receive dividends (barely anything) while having access to attend annual meetings as a shareholder. I could not believe it! As a sports fan, this was a great way to express my fandom. So I went ahead and purchased ten shares in Manchester United. As silly as it sounds, I partially represent the team. As someone who goes all in with whatever I get excited about, I certainly went all in with my fandom. I bought a jersey, I watch games, and I have sweatshirts and tee shirts that represent my passion and excitement for Manchester United. I am constantly keeping up with games, scores, and statistics after every game. I am sold out for Manchester United!

We all have the opportunity to decide to follow Jesus. This is not a decision that comes lightly. We don't just say we follow Jesus and all is said and done. When we decide to follow Jesus, the Spirit of the living God makes a home in us, and it is only the beginning of a kingdom life on earth. From that moment, we are made new. We are transformed. We are no longer who we once were. We were bought with a price, and we committed our lives to be in the family of God by way of Jesus. Who we once were is no longer who we aim to be. We are now representatives and ambassadors for Jesus. Our goal is to live for Jesus and make his name known to those around us. The Spirit of God gives us the ability to do just that. Our ability to surrender to the Spirit and trust that God will use the Spirit to represent himself through us is a humbling task. But this is what we are called to—offer the ministry of reconciliation to those around us. When Paul was writing his second letter to the church in Corinth, he wrote:

> From now on, then, we do not know anyone from a worldly perspective. Even if we have known Christ from a worldly perspective, yet now we no longer know him in this way. Therefore, if anyone is in Christ, he is a new creation; the old has passed away,

and see, the new has come! Everything is from God, who has reconciled us to himself through Christ and has given us the ministry of reconciliation. That is, in Christ, God was reconciling the world to himself, not counting their trespasses against them, and he has committed the message of reconciliation to us. Therefore, we are ambassadors for Christ, since God is making his appeal through us. We plead on Christ's behalf, "Be reconciled to God." He made the one who did not know sin to be sin for us, so that in him we might become the righteousness of God. (2 Cor 5:16–21)

Jesus Christ has revolutionized human history. In Christ, everything has changed. God is still using Jesus as the source of reconciling the world back to himself. As followers of Jesus, we serve as representatives, or ambassadors, of Christ and his kingdom. We get to put on our kingdom uniform and advocate for reconciliation. We have the privilege of living life on earth as it is in heaven by representing the person of Jesus. As we do this, it is important to not neglect the need for the Holy Spirit to aid us in the process. Jesus is the vine, and we are the branches. Apart from him, we are incapable. As John records Jesus's words in his Gospel, Jesus said, "I am the vine; you are the branches. The one who remains in me and I in him produces much fruit, because you can do nothing without me" (John 15:5). We can do nothing without Christ. We desperately need him. Jesus knew this, and this is why it was vital for him to send us his Spirit. His Spirit intercedes on our behalf. Just as Paul wrote to the church in Rome regarding prayer, the Spirit helps us in our weaknesses (Rom 8:26). Without Jesus being present in us through the Holy Spirit, we are weak. We are made strong in our weakness when we recognize our need for the Holy Spirit. When we represent Jesus, the Spirit can intercede on our behalf, giving us everything we need to make the name of Jesus known to the world around us. The Holy Spirit equips us to be faithful ambassadors.

PERSEVERING SPIRIT

I am not a runner. I repeat. I am not a runner. Far from it. I have a horrible relationship with cardio, and I know it is a problem. My wife, on the other hand, has enjoyed running her whole life. She signed up to run the Chicago Marathon in 2015. To this day, I am proud of her. But I remember when she was training for the marathon. Each day brought new challenges. Throughout the training, some aches and pains would come out of nowhere—but she persisted. With the goal in mind, it was enough to keep her going as she battled the challenge and the gradual increase in mileage in her training. After many long months of training, she was ready to take on the challenge of the marathon itself. By the way, I trained beside her, every step of the way. Except I rode a bicycle next to her while she ran. Together, we did it!

The Christian faith is a marathon. But much of it feels like training for one. Our spiritual formation on earth serves to prepare us for the glory of kingdom life. Along the way, we face a variety of aches and pains. Some days it feels like we are running more miles than anticipated as we attempt to grasp for air. Trials blast us out of nowhere, and we feel too weak and wounded to press on. We have days where we may feel like we are not going to be able to make it another day. We're tired. We're spent. We thirst. We long for nourishment and recovery so that we can be built up again.

This is a great time to be reminded of one of my favorite promises that comes from God. When Joshua took Moses's place in leading Israel, Moses offered Joshua a word of encouragement: "The Lord is the one who will go before you. He will be with you; he will not leave you or abandon you. Do not be afraid or discouraged" (Deut 31:8). God never abandons his people. God never breaks his promises. When we feel spent, exhausted, and parched, God reminds us that he never leaves us. He never abandons us. The Holy Spirit dwells in our midst and gives us the ability to prevail when we are weak and wounded. The Holy Spirit can fill us up to the point that our cup overflows with praise and thanksgiving. When we feel like we have nothing left to give, our response must be to drink deeply from the well of God's grace. It is in the grace of God that our souls receive everlasting nourishment. Our sustenance in the race of life does not come from overworking and over-performing; our sustenance comes from our dependence on the Holy Spirit. When we crave the Holy Spirit's presence, the Spirit will meet us and quench our thirst. We are not alone. We never have to be alone. The power and presence of God supplies us with the ability to have the necessary endurance to finish the race. The author of Hebrews reminds us of this:

> Our sustenance in the race of life does not come from overworking and over-performing; our sustenance comes from our dependence on the Holy Spirit.

> Therefore, since we also have such a large cloud of witnesses surrounding us, let us lay aside every hindrance and the sin that so easily ensnares us. Let us run with endurance the race that lies before us, keeping our eyes on Jesus, the pioneer and perfecter of our faith. For the joy that lay before him, he endured the cross, despising the shame, and sat down at the right hand of the throne of God. (Heb 12:1–2)

When we can keep our eyes on Jesus—who is the pioneer and perfecter of our faith—we will have everything we need to persevere with endurance. Jesus was the one who demonstrated the perfect form of endurance. He ran the race. He perfected the race. And he has given us an example of how to do the same. We can't persevere on our own. It is only when we give ourselves over to Jesus—relying on him for strength—that we can run the race. What a gift for followers of Jesus—the Holy Spirit. Relying on ourselves while running the race of the Christian faith will not prepare us to be kingdom people. Relying on Jesus Christ, who ran the race for us and showed us what dependence on God looked like, will prepare us for kingdom life on earth.

PROCESS AND REFLECT: KINGDOM SPIRIT

1. Do you believe that your life is truly led by the Spirit? Explain.
2. Where in your life do you feel like you don't depend on the Holy Spirit?
3. What adjustments can you make to live a more Spirit-filled life?
4. The Holy Spirit is the third person of the Trinity. Why do you think we often forget that the Spirit is vital in our lives?

CHAPTER 7

Kingdom Hope

Israel, put your hope in the Lord. For there is faithful love with the Lord, and with him is redemption in abundance.

—Ps 130:7

I AM AN AVID Chicago sports fan (minus the White Sox). I bleed Cubbie Blue. Michael Jordan is the best basketball player of all time—discussion over. The Chicago Bears, well, there is always next year. Being a sports fan can come with a roller coaster of emotions, especially if you are passionate. I remember growing up a Cubs fan, knowing that the Cubs had not won a World Series since 1908. Every time they gave a glimmer of hope, they would fail. It was this ongoing cycle of hoping the year would finally come when the Cubs would win the World Series, only to be disappointed yet again. Constant hope was given to the fandom, yet fans were let down, year after year. It was a perpetual cycle of hopelessness. As you may know, the Chicago Cubs had a historic run in 2016 and finished the year off with their first World Series championship since 1908. That's right, it took the Cubs 108 years to achieve what fans had been longing for all along. It was a joyous day when the final out was made. Hope had arrived. But it was temporary. Going into the following season, the Cubs had high expectations to do what they had proven they could do—win. It was a season where they fell short of the goal. The following year, the narrative remained the same. All of a sudden this team that was so successful, a team that had brought hope to the city of Chicago, found itself stumbling. Eventually, the team entered into a rebuild, and the championship roster was dismantled.

The problem with hope when it comes to sports is that it does not last. It is a temporary hope. You live it up in the moment, and then it fades away. In these situations, hope can be overpromised and under delivered. When it comes to kingdom hope, it is hope that is eternal. It is never ending. God gives us hope that never fails. He has a proven track record of this kind of hope. When Adam and Eve participated in bringing sin into the world, the world was not without hope. God had a plan of restoration and redemption (Gen 3:15). Following this, the world continued to grow in wickedness and evil (Gen 6:5), and God was grieved (Gen 6:6). Even still, God provided a way. God made a covenant with Noah (Gen 9). God told Noah, "This is the sign of the covenant I am making between me and you and every living creature with you, a covenant for all future generations: I have placed my bow in the clouds, and it will be a sign of the covenant between me and the earth" (Gen 9:12–13). God then made a covenant with Abram:

> The Lord said to Abram: Go from your land, your relatives, and your father's house to the land that I will show you. I will make you into a great nation, I will bless you, I will make your name great, and you will be a blessing. I will bless those who bless you, I will curse anyone who treats you with contempt, and all the peoples on earth will be blessed through you. (Gen 12:1–3)

This covenant between God and Abram seemed farfetched. Especially because Abram's wife, Sarah, was barren. Genesis puts it this way:

> "Where is your wife Sarah?" they asked him. "There, in the tent," he answered. The Lord said, "I will certainly come back to you in about a year's time, and your wife Sarah will have a son!" Now Sarah was listening at the entrance of the tent behind him. Abraham and Sarah were old and getting on in years. Sarah had passed the age of childbearing. So she laughed to herself: "After I am worn out and my lord is old, will I have delight?" But the Lord asked Abraham, "Why did Sarah laugh, saying, 'Can I really have a baby when I'm old?' Is anything impossible for the Lord? At the appointed time I will come back to you, and in about a year she will have a son." Sarah denied it. "I did not laugh," she said, because she was afraid. But he replied, "No, you did laugh." (Gen 18:9–15)

Sarah was laughing because of the ridiculous thought of being able to bear a child at such an old age. From her perspective, this seemed impossible.

But nothing is impossible for God. God makes promises and offers hope. His faithfulness is proven and true. Since he made a promise to Abram and Sarah, God was going to come through. The hopelessness of humanity is conquered by the hope that is found in God. We saw this unfold when God appeared to Sarah and fulfilled his promise. "The Lord came to Sarah as he had said, and the Lord did for Sarah what he had promised. Sarah became pregnant and bore a son to Abraham in his old age, at the appointed time God had told him. Abraham named his son who was born to him—the one Sarah bore to him—Isaac" (Gen 21:1–3). What seems hopeless in the eyes of humankind is never too much in the eyes of God. God, according to his plan and purpose, faithfully fills humanity with incomprehensible hope. He was faithful then, and he is faithful now. We can put our hope in God, because he has proven himself throughout the history of humanity. When everything around us seems hopeless, let us be assured that we can rest in the hope that God offers.

HOPE IN DEPENDENCE

When I read the psalms of ascent, I see people who know their God deeply and personally. They are eager to experience him and be in his presence as they journey to Jerusalem. Psalm 130 is an individual lament psalm that is filled with hope. The psalmist sings:

> Out of the depths I call to you, Lord!
> Lord, listen to my voice;
>   let your ears be attentive to my cry for help.
> Lord, if you kept an account of iniquities,
>   Lord, who could stand?
> But with you there is forgiveness,
>   so that you may be revered.
> I wait for the Lord; I wait and put my hope in his word.
> I wait for the Lord more than watchmen for the morning—more
> than watchmen for the morning.
> Israel, put your hope in the Lord.
>   For there is faithful love with the Lord, and with him is redemption
>   in abundance.
>   And he will redeem Israel from all its iniquities. (Ps 130)

The psalmist begins with a cry to the Lord. This cry demonstrates the psalmist's hope in the Lord. Verses 1–2 specifically show that God brings us from self-sufficiency to complete reliance. There is a cry of dependence. The psalmist is not trying to figure out his life on his own. The desire is for the Lord to listen to his voice and to be attentive to his cry for help.

We tend to be self-sufficient. We want to do things on our own. When it comes to our faith, we try to do more and be better, so that we can become *better Christians*. We try and try, and even on our best days, it is still not good enough for God. This is why Jesus came. Jesus is perfect for us so that we don't have to be. The psalmist realized that he could not be self-sufficient in this thing called life. He needed to rely and depend completely on God. We were not created to be self-sufficient people either. We were created to be dependent on our Creator. Putting our hope in God means that we are releasing control and completely relying on him for every outcome. The psalmist is in despair. The psalmist desires that the Lord would hear his cry for help. His dependence is completely given over to God, because on his own, he cannot make it. Transformational hope can be experienced when we surrender our dependence of self upon the Lord. Dependence on God will give us the confidence we need to rest in his promises.

> *Putting our hope in God means that we are releasing control and completely relying on him for every outcome.*

> *Dependence on God will give us the confidence we need to rest in his promises.*

HOPE IN FORGIVENESS

Many of us inevitably live with guilt, shame, remorse, and regret. There are things which we need to make peace with and move on from. But there is still a tendency to feel like we are not good enough for God to accept us. We feel like we owe something to God, and then perhaps he will accept us into his family. But God has already come up with a solution that welcomes us into his eternal kingdom family. That solution is Jesus. Jesus paved the way for us to experience forgiveness for our sins. Our guilt, shame, remorse, and regret are nailed to the cross, and we are set free by the broken body and shed blood of Jesus. We can release our burdens to Jesus, and he will take them upon himself. We can rest in these promises, because God takes us from guilt to forgiveness.

Kingdom Formation

The psalmist sings, "Lord, if you kept an account of iniquities, Lord, who could stand? But with you there is forgiveness, so that you may be revered" (Ps 130:3–4). As we live in our past guilt or our current sin patterns, it is easy for us to get caught up in the shame of it all. The psalmist does a great job of portraying the power of God's forgiveness. We don't have to ruminate on the weight of our past, because we have hope for our future. The Lord does not keep a record of our wrongs. If he did, no one could stand. With God, there is forgiveness, so that he may be revered. God forgives us for our wrongdoings. He forgives us for our sins. He does this through the person of Jesus. When we receive Jesus as our Lord and Savior, we are saved from the wickedness of our past, present, and future mistakes. As we begin to understand the depths of God's love through the person of Jesus, a kingdom response would be to fall on our knees and worship. This is what the psalmist is trying to demonstrate. God does not keep account of our iniquities, so let us revere God! Let us shout praises because of the hope that is found in Christ. We are a free people who are no longer defined by our sins. So we must respond with praise. Being formed for the kingdom will deepen our longing and desire to praise God in all of life's circumstances, because we have hope in Jesus. This is the natural outpouring of who we are because of what Christ did for us. This is not something that comes easily. We don't naturally pause to praise God on our own doing. This is why we so desperately need to rely on the Holy Spirit to enable us to praise God in all that we do. A posture such as this is what it would look like to bring the kingdom of heaven down to earth. An earthly version of the kingdom would be saturated with praise and worship of the Lord. Eternity itself will be filled with worship and praise. John writes this in Revelation:

> I looked, and there was a vast multitude from every nation, tribe, people, and language, which no one could number, standing before the throne and before the Lamb. They were clothed in white robes with palm branches in their hands. And they cried out in a loud voice:
> Salvation belongs to our God, who is seated on the throne, and to the Lamb!

> *As we begin to understand the depths of God's love through the person of Jesus, a kingdom response would be to fall on our knees and worship.*

Kingdom Hope

> All the angels stood around the throne, and along with the elders and the four living creatures they fell facedown before the throne and worshiped God, saying,
>
> Amen! Blessing and glory and wisdom and thanksgiving and honor and power and strength be to our God forever and ever. Amen. (Rev 7:9–12)

This is a powerful picture of what eternal worship looks like. But eternity does not have to begin when our life on earth is over. Eternity begins the moment we receive Jesus as our Lord and Savior. After our salvation, we can experience glimpses of eternity through our relationship with Jesus. We can witness communal worship when we gather each week as followers of Jesus. We see God at work in our lives and in the lives of those around us. We see people healed. We see lives transformed. We experience the person of Jesus being shared with others while their lives are transformed by the work of the Holy Spirit. We can catch glimpses of the things that God is doing for eternity here on earth, each day. What a joy it is to participate in kingdom life on earth. All of this is possible because the God who made the heavens and the earth has redeemed us by the blood of his Son, Jesus Christ. We are forgiven. We have hope in the goodness of God here on earth. Lean in and receive this hope. Even when the world may be hurting, God is restoring lives to himself. This is the power of hope. God will give us renewed strength and resilience. As David writes in Psalms, "The Lord is my strength and my shield; my heart trusts in him, and I am helped. Therefore my heart celebrates, and I give thanks to him with my song. The Lord is the strength of his people; he is a stronghold of salvation for his anointed" (Ps 28:7–8).

HOPE IN THE WAITING

We can all agree that waiting is challenging. If you think otherwise, I would love to get to know you so that you can educate me on how fun it is to wait in life. When we approach our spiritual formation through the lens of kingdom hope, the power of the Holy Spirit turns our waiting into assurance. The opposite is felt among many. We wait and we wait and we wait. The longer we wait, the more hopeless we feel. When it comes to our faith journey, waiting on God does not always mean that God will give us what we are waiting for. Sometimes waiting on God means that he uses our waiting to grow our assurance in him and his purposes for us. The psalmist gives us a glimpse into what waiting on the Lord looks like and where we can ground our hope while we wait: "I wait for the Lord; I wait and put my hope in his word. I wait for the Lord more than watchmen for the morning—more than watchmen for the morning" (Ps 130:5–6). The psalmist can find assurance in God's word while waiting. The Hebrew word here for "word" is *dābār*, which is literally translated as "a saying or utterance."[1] This means that the psalmist can find hope in the words that come from God while waiting. As mentioned earlier, there is hope in God and his word. God is faithful, and he always gives us a strong foundation to root ourselves in. When everything else around us feels shaky, God can root us on solid ground. That solid ground, of course, is the cornerstone—Jesus. While we wait for God, we can be assured by the promises that are made to us in Christ. Jesus offers us salvation. Jesus offers us forgiveness. Jesus offers us kingdom life on earth when we give ourselves to him. We can also be assured that while we find ourselves in the waiting, God promises to be in it with us. We will never be left alone or abandoned. That is the beauty of a faithful Savior who cares for his people. Jesus is the chief shepherd who never abandons his wandering sheep. As we wait upon the Lord, let us remember to wait with our hope grounded in the person of Jesus and the truth of God's word.

> *Jesus is the chief shepherd who never abandons his wandering sheep.*

HOPE IN REDEMPTION

In the Christian faith, Jesus is everything. If Jesus was not resurrected from the dead, then the Christian faith is pointless. Paul tells this to the church in Corinth. Paul writes, "If there is no resurrection of the dead, then not even Christ has been raised; and if Christ has not been raised, then our proclamation is in vain, and so is your faith" (1 Cor 15:13–14). But praise be to God that this is not the case. We have hope because of the redemption that is given to us in Christ Jesus. Paul declares this beautiful truth to the church in Corinth, "But as it is, Christ has been raised from the dead, the firstfruits of those who have fallen asleep. For since death came through a man, the resurrection of the dead also comes through a man. For just as in Adam all die, so also in Christ all will be made alive" (1 Cor 15:20–22). Followers of Jesus are made alive in him. He redeems the lost and broken

---

1. See https://www.blueletterbible.org/lexicon/h1697/csb/wlc/0-1/.

and gives them new life in himself. This is good news! Typically, when we receive good news we desire to share it with others.

In 2012, I decided to propose to my then-girlfriend. We both went to downtown Chicago to one of our favorite locations—North Avenue Beach. When you walk out on the pier of North Avenue Beach, there is a nice view of the Chicago skyline. I thought it would make for a nice picture for our engagement. I had asked a private photographer to be present at three o'clock (which was the time I planned to propose). As we made our way to the pier, I noticed that the photographers were already there and they were trying to blend in, not giving away their identity. As my girlfriend and I approached the pier, she jokingly made a comment and said, "Those people are being really weird with their camera, pretend to get down on your knee and propose to me." I could not believe what I just heard. I was given a cue to propose. So guess what? I did it. Right then and there. I got down on one knee and asked the magic question: "Will you marry me?" She said yes! The photographers captured the whole thing, and it made for a very magical day. Soon after the proposal, my new fiancée and I could not help but share the news with everyone we interacted with. We told random people on the streets of Chicago. We called our family and friends and shared the news. We were so excited that we could not contain it within ourselves.

As kingdom people, we have the best news that we can receive. Jesus Christ came into a broken world and offered his life so that we could have life everlasting. He redeemed us and restored us into the kingdom family. Redemption is offered to all. It is a free gift that Jesus gives at the cost of himself. Putting our hope in Jesus reveals our need for redemption. We recognize that without Christ we are lost and hopeless. The psalmist realized the power of putting hope in God. He benefited from experiencing what God was capable of doing. This is what the psalmist sang: "Israel, put your hope in the Lord. For there is faithful love with the Lord, and with him is redemption in abundance. And he will redeem Israel from all its iniquities" (Ps 130:7–8). The psalmist had the desire that Israel would recognize the abundance that was offered in the Lord's redemption. It was life changing. God's faithful love gives access to redemption from all iniquities. The psalmist had news that could not be withheld. The Lord's redeeming love powerfully transformed the lives of many. Israel needed to hear this good news. The psalmist made it a point to make sure the good news was shared and spread so that lives would be transformed.

KINGDOM HOPE

Hope is a powerful asset. Many have a difficult time experiencing hope in their lives. The more conversations I have with people, the more it feels like people are stuck in cycles of hopelessness. Or, their hope is simply put in the wrong places. It is placed in people and things that will always let them down. Followers of Jesus have access to kingdom hope. This hope starts with Jesus and ends with Jesus. Jesus paid it all, and all to him we owe.[2] He laid down his life for us because of his love. John records Jesus saying, "I am the good shepherd. The good shepherd lays down his life for the sheep" (John 10:11). That he faithfully did. Jesus laying down his life for us is why we can have kingdom hope. A hope that is not focused on what this world has to offer us. A hope that is not stuck in the media and politics. This hope is eternal. It is a hope that starts and finishes with a mindset that is fixed on the kingdom of God. The eternal kingdom is something that followers of Jesus look forward to. But I believe that followers of Jesus have access to the kingdom on earth. If Jesus dwells within the very being of who we are, then the kingdom has come down. Jesus alone defines what the kingdom of God is. He did this throughout his life. He taught us how to live. He taught us how to love. He taught us how to obey. He taught us how to care. He taught us how to do life with others. He taught us how to treat our enemies. He taught us how to prioritize the needs of others before our own. And most of all—he taught us how to sacrifice.

Our spiritual formation is vital. Who we become on earth prepares us for a kingdom life. The problem we face is that we like to take matters into our own hands and develop a lifestyle that attempts to replicate the life of Jesus. In this endeavor, we are confronted with sin, and this can lead us to a Pharisaical lifestyle. We can easily judge others who don't measure up to our standards and our understanding of who God is. We must swallow our pride and receive the humility of Jesus. Jesus alone can transform lives. Not us. God can use us as vessels, but we don't transform lives. It is by the work of the Holy Spirit that Christ Jesus so graciously gave us that we can be a mouthpiece for God and his kingdom. Our hope is in Jesus. When we surrender ourselves to Jesus, kingdom hope manifests itself in our lives. The call to kingdom living on earth as it is in heaven means that we humbly offer ourselves to Christ's care and trust that he will take care of the rest.

---

2. "Jesus paid it all, / All to Him I owe" goes the refrain from an old hymn. See Hall, "I Hear the Savior Say."

Transformation is a powerful demonstration of spiritual growth. Let us be transformed for life on earth as it is in heaven.

PROCESS AND REFLECT: KINGDOM HOPE

1. Why do you think this world does a poor job of offering hope?
2. What are some false hopes which you may have the tendency to cling to?
3. How can you apply kingdom hope to your life?
4. What can you do to intentionally share kingdom hope with those in your spheres of influence?
5. How has hope in Jesus changed your life?

CHAPTER 8

Kingdom Growth

Remain in me, and I in you. Just as a branch is unable to produce fruit by itself unless it remains on the vine, neither can you unless you remain in me. I am the vine; you are the branches. The one who remains in me and I in him produces much fruit, because you can do nothing without me.

—JOHN 15:4–5

WHEN I WAS DOING my undergraduate work at Moody Bible Institute, I picked up a job working in the landscaping department. Going into it, I knew nothing. Everything about landscaping was new to me, and I had to be trained significantly. After a while, I started to pick up on the basics of landscaping, even though there was so much more to learn. When my wife and I finally bought our first home, it was *our* home. It was exciting to be able to take care of our own place. Part of the work that needed to be done was landscaping work. Again, I knew the basics—how bad can it be? Well, during the fall, leaves fell all over our yard. I raked the leaves up in piles and left them as the weather got increasingly cold. Snow came, and the winter season came. I forgot I had ever done anything outdoors with the leaves. Until spring came. When the snow melted, I realized the piles of leaves had remained in their location. I figured I would go and rake them up again—this time with the intent of throwing them out. So I did just that. Except I ran into a problem. The three piles of leaves that were sitting on my nice grass had ended up killing the grass that they were lying on. My yard was filled with mostly green grass that was now accompanied by three large-sized patches of dirt. I went to the store and purchased grass seed, spread it around, and religiously watered the grass each day. I knew at that point all I could do was hope and wait. I did not have control over the outcome of how the grass would grow or how it would come in. What I could do consistently is water it. Some days, birds would come by and pick at the grass seed. On other days, the rain would come and take care of the grass-watering. Eventually, the grass began to come in and fill the dry dirt patches. The way that my yard was supposed to look was slowly coming to be. It looked new and fresh. There was life again.

In our endeavor to become people who live for the kingdom here on earth, we can fall into the trap of experiencing dry patches in our lives. There can seem to be a drought in our spiritual life. When this happens, how do we respond? Do we embrace and live in the dry patches of our spiritual formation, or do we seek sustenance that can only be provided by the source of living water himself—Jesus? Life is filled with seasons. There are many good seasons, and there are many bad seasons. In every season of life, we have unique opportunities to be formed by God. In our pain and sorrow, God is forming us. In our joy and celebration, God is forming us. For everything in between, God is forming us. This is all part of our sanctification—or our growth process. Every one of us is a work in progress until the Lord is finished with us and we arrive in the kingdom. Our spiritual development comes from Jesus who alone is our source of living water. Jesus is the one who fills us up when we are thirsty and depleting in our spiritual formation. Jesus is the true vine who produces kingdom fruit in us and gives us the ability to grow when we remain in him.

> *Jesus is the true vine who produces kingdom fruit in us and gives us the ability to grow when we remain in him.*

THE VINE AND THE BRANCHES

As followers of Jesus, we must continue to grow in our spiritual walk with Jesus. The more we grow, the more we live like kingdom people. We are unable to achieve this growth on our own. It is only by the grace of God and the strength of Christ that we are able to bear fruit in our spiritual journey.

Kingdom Formation

The Gospel writer John records a statement by Jesus as Jesus is teaching his disciples. Here is what John records:

> I am the true vine, and my Father is the gardener. Every branch in me that does not produce fruit he removes, and he prunes every branch that produces fruit so that it will produce more fruit. You are already clean because of the word I have spoken to you. Remain in me, and I in you. Just as a branch is unable to produce fruit by itself unless it remains on the vine, neither can you unless you remain in me. I am the vine; you are the branches. The one who remains in me and I in him produces much fruit, because you can do nothing without me. If anyone does not remain in me, he is thrown aside like a branch and he withers. They gather them, throw them into the fire, and they are burned. If you remain in me and my words remain in you, ask whatever you want and it will be done for you. My Father is glorified by this: that you produce much fruit and prove to be my disciples. (John 15:1–8)

When Jesus was communicating to his disciples, the message he was trying to get across to them was that he was their source and sustenance. Apart from him, they can do nothing. Jesus's charge was for his disciples to remain in him, because if they do not remain in him they will not be able to produce fruit. Fruit can be produced only when Jesus is the true vine. If the disciples were to not prioritize Jesus as their true vine, their ministry would be fruitless. When Jesus came onto the scene and began his earthly ministry, the one thing that he offered to those he encountered was himself. If people received Jesus, they would receive an everlasting flow of nourishment in their lives. They would have all they needed.

Jesus is the central source of our spiritual formation. He gets all of the credit when we grow in our faith journey. Apart from Jesus, we would just be withering branches that are drying up. When we make Jesus our true vine, we become branches that bear fruit for the kingdom. Fruit that edifies and strengthens us personally and fruit that is able to impact the lives of those around us. As followers of Jesus who bear good fruit, we are given the means to love others well. This is how the world will know that we are kingdom people. We are known that we belong to Jesus by our love (John 13:35). When God does a work in our hearts, we are then able to offer our new selves to those around us. This is how our growth in Jesus unfolds.

KINGDOM GROWTH

Our personal spiritual formation is our discipleship. It is how we are formed and molded to look more like followers of Jesus. Much of this book has focused on our own spiritual formation, giving us practical tools to utilize for growth in Christ. Growth is not easy. But growth is the challenge that is set before us. As disciples of Jesus, we are to live in his grace while submitting to his teachings. When we do this, the Holy Spirit will guide us and form us into who we were created to be. Our souls will be renewed. Our life will receive purpose and meaning. We will have strong instruction on how to live in the presence of God as we care for a broken and hurting world. Through this, we will grow. We will continue to grow. And when we grow, we can include others in that growth. Those in our inner and outer circles will get to participate in how God is molding us into kingdom people simply through our influence, because we've been immersed in Jesus. Our lives will serve as a living testimony to a world that is in desperate need of hope. Being a kingdom person means that we are bearers of hope due to the light that is in us. This light is not something we obtain simply by following the proper rules. This light is obtained by giving ourselves over to the King of eternity. King Jesus is the only one who can deepen our understanding of where we need to go and how we need to get there. Let us be a people who are intentional in pursuing Jesus. The more we pursue Jesus, the more we become like Jesus. The more we become like Jesus, the more we become a kingdom people.

As we seek to become more like Jesus, we must have the posture of a disciple—a student of Jesus. Our openness to receive from Jesus is crucial in our spiritual development. Being a student of Jesus means that we lay our presuppositions aside and have an open heart for what God is capable of doing in our lives. Our spiritual growth can be suppressed by our small view of God. Our theological framework and understanding are not infinite. In fact, our theological framework and understanding are finite. God has revealed everything we need to know about himself. God has given us the ability to understand the person of Jesus, who eternally saves us into the kingdom, where he will rule as Lord. There are many other theological truths that are revealed to us that are understandable. But as finite human beings, we cannot fully comprehend the depths of who God is. To better understand this, we must look at the enemy in the garden and see how there is a tendency to manipulate human beings into fully knowing God:

> Now the serpent was the most cunning of all the wild animals that the Lord God had made. He said to the woman, "Did God really say, 'You can't eat from any tree in the garden'?" The woman said to the serpent, "We may eat the fruit from the trees in the garden. But about the fruit of the tree in the middle of the garden, God said, 'You must not eat it or touch it, or you will die.'" "No! You will certainly not die," the serpent said to the woman. "In fact, God knows that when you eat it your eyes will be opened and you will be like God, knowing good and evil." (Gen 3:1–5)

There is a lot going on in this interaction, but the enemy's focus is *deception*. The crafty enemy was able to mislead humanity into thinking that they could know what God knows and be like God. There was a very clear temptation to know the things that God knew, so steps were taken to aquire that knowledge. Of course, it is impossible to fully know the depths of who God is. God has revealed everything to us in the person of Jesus. When we know Jesus, we know God. The Gospel writer John gives us a wonderful understanding of the person of Jesus:

> In the beginning was the Word, and the Word was with God, and the Word was God. He was with God in the beginning. All things were created through him, and apart from him not one thing was created that has been created. In him was life, and that life was the light of men. That light shines in the darkness, and yet the darkness did not overcome it. There was a man sent from God whose name was John. He came as a witness to testify about the light, so that all might believe through him. He was not the light, but he came to testify about the light. The true light that gives light to everyone was coming into the world. He was in the world, and the world was created through him, and yet the world did not recognize him. He came to his own, and his own people did not receive him. But to all who did receive him, he gave them the right to be children of God, to those who believe in his name, who were born, not of natural descent, or of the will of the flesh, or of the will of man, but of God. The Word became flesh and dwelt among us. We observed his glory, the glory as the one and only Son from the Father, full of grace and truth. (John 1:1–14)

Jesus is everything. Jesus is primary. He is the source of everything, and everything is for him. When we make it about us or when we think that we have figured everything out about God—there is a lot of work that needs to be done. Kingdom growth does not occur from us knowing everything; kingdom growth occurs when we humbly realize that we have a lot more left to learn. When we are rooted, grounded, and surrendered in a posture of humility, kingdom growth will follow.

HUMILITY PROPELS KINGDOM GROWTH

One of the most important things for kingdom formation is our humility. Kingdom growth begins and ends with humility. When humility is at our core, we become moldable. God is able to do far more with a person who is humble,vulnerable, and receptive than with one who is arrogant, prideful, and closed off. So in order for us to live this life on earth with a healthy desire for kingdom growth, we must seek the person of Jesus, who is able to equip us with the humility we need. Jesus is able to do this because he is the very definition of humility. When Paul was writing his letter to the church in Philippi, he wrote this:

> If, then, there is any encouragement in Christ, if any consolation of love, if any fellowship with the Spirit, if any affection and mercy, make my joy complete by thinking the same way, having the same love, united in spirit, intent on one purpose. Do nothing out of selfish ambition or conceit, but in humility consider others as more important than yourselves. Everyone should look not to his own interests, but rather to the interests of others. Adopt the same attitude as that of Christ Jesus, who, existing in the form of God, did not consider equality with God as something to be exploited. Instead he emptied himself by assuming the form of a servant, taking on the likeness of humanity. And when he had come as a man, he humbled himself by becoming obedient to the point of death—even to death on a cross. For this reason God highly exalted him and gave him the name that is above every name, so that at the name of Jesus every knee will bow—in heaven and on earth and under the earth—and every tongue will confess that Jesus Christ is Lord, to the glory of God the Father. (Phil 2:1–11)

Much of humility is a self-emptying love. It is a posture that does not do things out of selfish ambition. Imagine if Jesus lived a selfish life, making everything all about him and not others. Things may have turned out a little differently than they did. Instead, Jesus knew the life that he was called to live. He lived his life in obedience and trust, knowing that the will of God was to be sought after. In emptying himself, Jesus was able to bring glory to God. Through Jesus's acts of humility, all of humanity has been given the opportunity to receive everlasting life. Even though Jesus is God, Jesus did

Kingdom Formation

not consider equality with God as something to be exploited. Jesus took on the identity of suffering servant as his way of demonstrating humility and love to the world. Jesus's glory stems from his humility.

The practice of love and humility in our lives replicates who Jesus was and is in his very nature. We become more Christlike when we become a people of humility. Humility is not an abstract thought. Humility is an ongoing indicator of a heart that longs to be transformed by the gospel. As followers of Jesus, we experience humility in our lives the more we strive for Jesus and Jesus alone. Andrew Murray once wrote:

> *Humility is an ongoing indicator of a heart that longs to be transformed by the gospel.*

> The life of those who are saved, the saints, must bear this stamp of deliverance from sin and full restoration to their original state; their whole relationship to God and to man marked by an all-pervading humility. Without this there can be no true abiding in God's presence or experience of his favor and the power of the Holy Spirit; without this no abiding faith or love or joy or strength. Humility is the only soil in which virtue takes root; a lack of humility is the explanation of every defect and failure. Humility is not so much a virtue along with the others, but is the root of all, because it alone takes the right attitude before God and allows him, as God, to do all.[1]

A lifestyle that demonstrates humility is a lifestyle that pursues holiness. Holiness is not something that we accomplish by achieving tasks for the kingdom—no, holiness is something that Christ does in us the more we pursue him. The scribes and the Pharisees were people who sought to become holy by upholding their religiosity. Jesus came and squashed their perception of holiness by calling them out for their acts of self-righteous pursuits. Self-righteousness is not the way to holiness, as so often can be perceived and represented among believers. The way to holiness is through the embodiment of Christlike humility. The power of humility in us means that we may not know everything, and that is okay. What we need to know is who Jesus is and what Jesus says. Humility can be a challenging character trait to obtain—especially with one's own efforts—but this is why we look to the person of Jesus to help us form a life of humility. When we do, we will experience kingdom growth.

---

1. Murray, *Humility*, 17.

KINGDOM GROWTH THROUGH JESUS

Becoming more like Jesus is the most important element of kingdom formation. Jesus did things that none of us could ever do. Particularly, Jesus ushered in the kingdom of God into the very world that was created by God. There is a beautiful paradox in the collision of heaven and earth. Once perfect, the earth became broken and was in desperate need of redemption and healing. God incarnated himself in the person of Jesus to demonstrate to this world just how majestic and tender our God is. There was majesty in Jesus because he was to be the King of kings and Lord of lords (Rev 19:16). He is the one who is worthy of all our worship. We bow before our King and surrender ourselves because he is glorious and mighty. Jesus is our victorious King who has conquered sin and death, once and for all (1 Cor 15:54–57). At the same time, this Jesus is tender. This majestic King is filled with compassion for his people (Matt 9:36; 14:14; Mark 6:34). He understands his people. He is burdened by the burdens of his people. When Jesus feels compassion toward his people he responds to that compassion with action. He intentionally looks to meet the needs of his flock, nurturing them with his everlasting presence and power. Most importantly, this King Jesus is recklessly in love with the people of this broken and hurting world (John 3:16–18). Jesus gave his life for us so that we would live in him. What a beautiful gift! Deciding to follow Jesus means that we are looking to grow in our spiritual formation through the nourishment that comes from the broken body and shed blood of Christ. Jesus took our sin upon himself because we were a helpless people in need of saving. There is nothing that we can do apart from the strength of Jesus in our lives. We must depend on Jesus. We must rely on Jesus. We must trust in Jesus. We must give ourselves over to Jesus every single day. And when it comes to our spiritual formation, sure, we can do things that help aid and assist our growth with Jesus, but it is Jesus alone who does the growth. Let us rest in the grace and goodness of Jesus, giving him room to mold us and shape us into kingdom people.

    The other portion of kingdom growth comes through the community of other kingdom people. Since followers of Jesus will dwell together in unity in the eternal kingdom, we must long to replicate this kingdom on earth through our communal fellowship. Kingdom growth cannot be achieved or accomplished on our own. We need to be challenged in our spiritual formation and grow in Jesus, but we also need to find growth in our spiritual formation through the relationships which God has wired us for. When we are bound to Jesus, we are bound to the people of God. Jesus uniquely manifests himself through our participation in community with one another.

Kingdom growth happens when our earthly nature collides with the paradox of kingdom come. In this, we surrender what we understand to be normal and embrace the mysteries of who God is and what God is uniquely doing in the life of his bride, the church. With Jesus being Lord and Ruler of his church, the church is able to experience kingdom come. This is where transformation happens. This is where lives are changed and people thrive. As followers of Jesus, let us cling to him, and he will pierce our hearts with the kingdom. When we faithfully express this posture, Jesus will take us on a journey of personal and communal spiritual formation that will bolster our spiritual vitality for kingdom growth. He will give us the ability to thrive not by our own doing but by our learning to rely on his completed work on the cross. Will you respond to the invitation? The invitation set before us is to simply come. Come as you are. Enter into the loving arms of Jesus, and watch what Jesus can do in your life. May the kingdom of God take root in the very being of who you are, and may the person of Jesus shape you into who you were created to be—a kingdom-formed child of the living God.

PROCESS AND REFLECT: KINGDOM GROWTH

1. On a scale of one to ten, where are you in regard to your spiritual growth?
2. What needs to change to help facilitate further growth?
3. What is the biggest challenge with humility in your life?
4. What are things that you need to get rid of in your life that will help you become a person of kingdom humility?

Epilogue

This kingdom of God life is not a matter of waking up each morning with a list of chores or an agenda to be tended to, left on our bedside table by the Holy Spirit for us while we slept. We wake up already immersed in a large story of creation and covenant, of Israel and Jesus, the story of Jesus and the stories that Jesus told. We let ourselves be formed by these formative stories, and especially as we listen to the stories that Jesus tells, get a feel for the way he does it, the way he talks, the way he treats people, the Jesus way.[1]

—Eugene Peterson, *Tell It Slant*

What a journey it has been. Thank you for giving your time and reading this book. We have ventured through a plethora of ideas, concepts, and principles for our own personal growth and spiritual formation. My heart and passion behind this book rests completely in the fact that I want to see followers of Jesus truly be transformed. I desire to see the spiritual temperature in the lives of believers hit an all-time high. How amazing would it be if followers of Jesus were known and recognized for their love of God and love of people? This would truly transform our homes, our neighborhoods, our communities, and our world. I believe this because I believe in the God of the universe who incarnated himself into human form and lived a perfect and spotless life. Who willingly gave himself to us so that we would have eternal life in him. Jesus was raised from the dead and defeated sin and death, once and for all. This is Jesus—the one who loves and cares for his creation. All of creation groans at the pain and suffering that surrounds

---

1. Peterson, *Tell It Slant*, 154.

Kingdom Formation

it. But Jesus came to bring hope. We have the opportunity to invite this Jesus to be our Lord and King. When we do, we cannot possibly be the same. If Jesus has truly gotten a hold of our hearts and replaced all other gods and idols in our lives, then our lives will demonstrate an outpouring of kingdom life on earth. The question for us is this: Are we being formed for kingdom life on earth as it is in heaven? Eugene Peterson states it best:

> This kingdom of God life is not a matter of waking up each morning with a list of chores or an agenda to be tended to, left on our bedside table by the Holy Spirit for us while we slept. We wake up already immersed in a large story of creation and covenant, of Israel and Jesus, the story of Jesus and the stories that Jesus told. We let ourselves be formed by these formative stories, and especially as we listen to the stories that Jesus tells, get a feel for the way he does it, the way he talks, the way he treats people, the Jesus way.[2]

Kingdom life means that we commit ourselves to the story that God is writing. God has written a profound story of redemption from Genesis to Revelation. But his story is not finished yet. You are part of what he is doing for the eternal kingdom. But the eternal kingdom does not start when our life on earth is over. The eternal kingdom starts when we give our life over to Jesus. If you have given your life over to Jesus, you are living kingdom life. You are operating with the power of the Holy Spirit. God is within you. Think about that! He is miraculously residing in your very being so that you may be able to be his ambassador for kingdom life on earth. Take a deep breath. Breathe in the grace of God. He is for you. He is with you. Now go and be Jesus in your context, and see how the Spirit of the living God transforms you for kingdom life on earth as it is in heaven. May you rest in these words from Paul:

> For this reason also, since the day we heard this, we haven't stopped praying for you. We are asking that you may be filled with the knowledge of his will in all wisdom and spiritual understanding, so that you may walk worthy of the Lord, fully pleasing to him: bearing fruit in every good work and growing in the knowledge of God, being strengthened with all power, according to his glorious might, so that you may have great endurance and patience, joyfully giving thanks to the Father, who has enabled you to share in the saints' inheritance in the light. He has rescued us from the

---

2. Peterson, *Tell It Slant*, 154.

Epilogue

domain of darkness and transferred us into the kingdom of the Son he loves. In him we have redemption, the forgiveness of sins. (Col 1:9–14).

Praise be to God.

Biblical Texts for Further Study on the Kingdom

But seek first the kingdom of God and his righteousness, and all these things will be provided for you.

—Matt 6:33

For the kingdom of God is not eating and drinking, but righteousness, peace, and joy in the Holy Spirit.

—Rom 14:17

Therefore I tell you, the kingdom of God will be taken away from you and given to a people producing its fruit.

—Matt 21:43

The time is fulfilled, and the kingdom of God has come near. Repent and believe the good news!

—Mark 1:15

Blessed are the poor in spirit, for the kingdom of heaven is theirs.

—Matt 5:3

Blessed are those who are persecuted because of righteousness, for the kingdom of heaven is theirs.

—Matt 5:10

Biblical Texts for Further Study on the Kingdom

Therefore, you should pray like this: Our Father in heaven, your name be honored as holy. Your kingdom come. Your will be done on earth as it is in heaven.

—Matt 6:9–10

I tell you that many will come from east and west to share the banquet with Abraham, Isaac, and Jacob in the kingdom of heaven.

—Matt 8:11

Jesus continued going around to all the towns and villages, teaching in their synagogues, preaching the good news of the kingdom, and healing every disease and every sickness.

—Matt 9:35

If I drive out demons by the Spirit of God, then the kingdom of God has come upon you.

—Matt 12:28

He presented another parable to them: "The kingdom of heaven is like a mustard seed that a man took and sowed in his field. It's the smallest of all the seeds, but when grown, it's taller than the garden plants and becomes a tree, so that the birds of the sky come and nest in its branches."

—Matt 13:31–32

He told them another parable: "The kingdom of heaven is like leaven that a woman took and mixed into fifty pounds of flour until all of it was leavened."

—Matt 13:33

The kingdom of heaven is like treasure, buried in a field, that a man found and reburied. Then in his joy he goes and sells everything he has and buys that field.

—Matt 13:44

Kingdom Formation

Again, the kingdom of heaven is like a merchant in search of fine pearls. When he found one priceless pearl, he went and sold everything he had and bought it.

—Matt 13:45

Bibliography

Barry, John D., et al., eds. *Faithlife Study Bible*. Bellingham, WA: Lexham, 2016.
Beitzel, Barry J. "Zacchaeus." In *Baker Encyclopedia of the Bible*, edited by Walter A. Elwell, 2:2175. Grand Rapids: Baker, 1988.
Blum, Edwin A., and Trevin Wax, eds. *CSB Study Bible: Notes*. Nashville: Holman, 2017.
Bonhoeffer, Dietrich. *Life Together: The Classic Exploration of Christian Community*. Princeton, NJ: HarperOne, 1978.
Carson, D. A. *The Gospel According to John*. Pillar New Testament Commentary. Grand Rapids: Eerdmans, 1991.
Cole, R. Alan. *Mark: An Introduction and Commentary*. Tyndale New Testament Commentaries. Downers Grove, IL: InterVarsity, 1989.
Erickson, Millard J. *Christian Theology*. 3rd ed. Grand Rapids: Baker Academic, 2013.
ESV Study Bible. Illustrated ed. Wheaton, IL: Crossway, 2008.
Foster, Richard J. *Celebration of Discipline: The Path to Spiritual Growth*. Anniv. ed. San Francisco: HarperOne, 2018.
Hall, Elvina M. "I Hear the Savior Say, 'Thy Strength Indeed Is Small.'" Hymnary, 1865. https://hymnary.org/text/i_hear_the_savior_say_thy_strength_indee.
Hyun, Timothy. "Tabernacle." In *The Lexham Bible Dictionary*, edited by John D. Barry et al., n.p. Bellingham, WA: Lexham, 2016. Logos Bible software.
Keller, Timothy. *Prayer: Experiencing Awe and Intimacy with God*. New York: Penguin, 2016.
Kruse, Colin G. *John: An Introduction and Commentary*. Tyndale New Testament Commentaries. Downers Grove, IL: InterVarsity, 2003.
Logos Staff. "The Apostles' Creed: Its History and Origins." Logos, Jan. 18, 2022. Https://www.logos.com/grow/the-apostles-creed-its-history-and-origins/.
Marshall, I. Howard. *Acts: An Introduction and Commentary*. Tyndale New Testament Commentaries. Downers Grove, IL: InterVarsity, 1980.
Miller, Paul. *A Praying Life: Connecting with God in a Distracting World*. Colorado Springs, CO: NavPress, 2009.
Motyer, J. Alec. *Isaiah: An Introduction and Commentary*. Tyndale Old Testament Commentaries. Downers Grove, IL: InterVarsity, 1999.
Murray, Andrew. *Humility: The Journey toward Holiness*. Reprint, Minneapolis: Bethany, 2001.
Ortlund, Dane C. *Gentle and Lowly: The Heart of Christ for Sinners and Sufferers*. Wheaton, IL: Crossway, 2020.

Bibliography

Peterson, Eugene H. *A Long Obedience in the Same Direction: Discipleship in an Instant Society*. Downers Grove, IL: InterVarsity, 2021.

———. *Tell It Slant: A Conversation on the Language of Jesus in His Stories and Prayers*. Reprint. Grand Rapids: Eerdmans, 2012.

Richards, E. Randolph, and Brandon J. O'Brien. *Misreading Scripture with Western Eyes: Removing Cultural Blinders to Better Understand the Bible*. Downers Grove, IL: InterVarsity, 2012.

Rosner, Brian S., et al., eds. *New Dictionary of Biblical Theology: Exploring the Unity Diversity of Scripture*. Downers Grove, IL: IVP Academic, 2000.

Zondervan Academic. "Who Was Herod?" Bible Gateway Blog, Dec. 19, 2017. https://www.biblegateway.com/blog/2017/12/who-was-herod/.

www.ingramcontent.com/pod-product-compliance
Lightning Source LLC
Chambersburg PA
CBHW072151160426
43197CB00012B/2339